#BlessedMother

#BlessedMother

How to Follow, Share, and Defend Mary
in the World of Social Media

TOMMY TIGHE

Our Sunday Visitor
Huntington, Indiana

Our Sunday Visitor Publishing Division
Our Sunday Visitor, Inc.
200 Noll Plaza
Huntington, IN 46750
www.osv.com
1-800-348-2440

ISBN: 978-1-68192-418-2 (Inventory No. T2311)
1. YOUNG ADULT NONFICTION—Religion—Christianity.
2. RELIGION—Christian Theology—Mariology.
3. RELIGION—Christianity—Catholic.

eISBN: 978-1-68192-419-9
LCCN: 2020936369

Cover and interior design: Lindsey Riesen
Cover art: Restored Traditions

PRINTED IN THE UNITED STATES OF AMERICA

To Karen, James, Paul, Andy, Luke, and Charlie. Your love and encouragement are what push me forward each and every day.

Contents

Introduction

Mary Follows Back

Driving through the rugged terrain of Northern California on a family road trip back when I was a child, my family found ourselves in a pretty precarious situation. My father tightly gripped the steering wheel of his old Ford F-350, 25-foot trailer in tow, as we traveled down a steep mountain road in the middle of a blizzard. Just another typical "fun" family outing for the Tighes. As my dad desperately tried to keep the truck and trailer on a road he could no longer see, my mother and I noticed the crucifix hanging from the rearview mirror swinging wildly back and forth. Typically, as a kid, I would find peace in the midst of scary situations thanks to my parents telling me "everything was going to be okay." This time around, however, they were both as scared as I was.

Panicked that this might very well be the end, my mother thought to do the only thing that made sense given the circumstances: a family Rosary. She began to lead us in the prayer as my father continued the hard work of trying to keep us alive and get us safely to the bottom of this mountain.

And then, something happened.

As we started in on the first mystery of the Rosary, the crucifix stopped swaying back and forth and hung completely still. Despite the fact that the blizzard continued to swirl, despite the fact that the truck and trailer continued to slide, find its grip on the road, and slide again, despite the fact that the truck kept bouncing in and out of holes, off onto the shoulder and back onto the road just as it had been doing the entire time, the crucifix hung completely still as we prayed the Rosary and pleaded for our family to survive this harrowing journey.

We all immediately took notice. We didn't say anything about it out loud, but there was a sense hanging in the air that we all realized we were sharing some kind of moment, an experience of something big happening right then and there.

As we wrapped up the first mystery and moved on to the second, our prayers were answered by way of a huge truck with a snowplow pulling up alongside my dad's window.

"Need some help getting down?" the kind stranger asked.

Boy, did we.

This man, who probably hasn't thought twice about the incident since it took place, then proceeded to slowly guide us down the rest of the mountain road, getting us safely to the bottom just as we wrapped up our family prayer. There was no doubt for any of us that God heard our prayer and sent us help from heaven so we wouldn't end up there ourselves that day.

The kind stranger drove off, and we continued on our family road trip without the danger of death staring us in the face again. That experience has stuck with me, even all these years later. It's hard to doubt the love and care of the Blessed Virgin Mary, her divine Son, and all the saints in heaven after you've had an experience where you felt their assistance so vividly.

That Fateful Phone Call

Despite the powerful experience of Mary's intercession on our family road trip, throughout much of my life I didn't work hard to develop a relationship with Mary. I didn't read about the theology behind her role in the Church. I didn't really even pray the Rosary all that much, unless my mom was encouraging me to do so in a given situation. Much like I did with my own mother, I took Mary for granted. I expected her to be there to help me when I needed her and didn't pay her much attention outside of that.

As I grew up, went away to college, fell in love, and started my career, that didn't change all that much. While I continued going to Mass and valuing the cultural aspects of Catholicism, I didn't do much to grow in my faith in young adulthood. Life was going pretty smoothly, and I didn't think I had much need for God since I had everything all figured out. I graduated college early, wrapped up my graduate degree, fell in love and got engaged, and started a fantastic government job in the field I actually studied. Yep, I had everything under control and didn't have a care in the world.

About one month into my new job, however, all that changed.

My dad called me with a tone in his voice that I had never heard before.

"I need you to come home," he calmly demanded.

I was confused, both by his tone and his seemingly odd request, and asked him to fill me in on what was going on.

"It's your mom … "

I don't remember many of the specifics after that point in the conversation. I remember walking out of work without telling anyone where I was going. I remember calling my then-fiancée as I made a U-turn to get onto the freeway. I remember telling her through intense tears that my mom was dead.

It was a shocking loss. While my mom had dealt with illness throughout her life, we didn't expect anything like this. She wasn't slowly declining in health over time, she wasn't diagnosed with some terminal illness, she wasn't supposed to die.

Death doesn't care about those things, though. Mom was gone.

I had experienced death in my family before this (grandparents, aunts and uncles, and others), but nothing compares to losing your mother. Nothing compares to suddenly not being able to talk to the woman who raised you and kept you safe for your entire life, not being able to feel the love of her embrace even though you're well into your twenties. Nothing compares.

I grieved her death in a way that I now see was rather typical for a man my age. I held in my emotions, I fought back the tears, and I allowed anger to wash over me. I was angry at God, angry at everyone who made unhelpful comments about how she was "in a better place," and angry at my mom for being gone even though she obviously didn't have any say in the matter.

Anger is weird in that way. It's illogical, directed at people it shouldn't be, and completely absorbing. Through all the planning of her funeral, through all the casseroles brought over to help us feel better, through all the support of my close family, distant relatives, and friends, the anger reigned.

The night before her funeral, we prayed a Rosary together. I was still seeing red, and every attempt at consolation felt insincere. Oddly, I felt angry that other people were having an opportunity to mourn the loss of my mother in that moment. Unless you've had a loss like this, that may sound confusing, but in that moment, I felt like *I* should be getting to mourn my mother's death, and no one else had the right to do the same.

As we prayed the Rosary, I also felt angry at God. I didn't see a reason to even mumble the words as the beads slid through my fingers. And yet, I kept praying, recognizing my mother's love of the Rosary and feeling like I owed it to her.

And much like the immediate feeling of grace that came over my family in the Ford F-350 all those years before, I felt a wave of peace and joy supernaturally wash over me. I wasn't expecting it, I wasn't asking for it, yet it happened. As the beads continued to move through my fingers with each Hail Mary, a smile came to my face. I couldn't help it. I didn't really understand what was happening, but I felt happy. I felt joyful.

The anger melted away and was replaced by happiness, peace, and acceptance. It didn't make sense, but it felt really, *really* good.

In that moment, I embarked on a relationship with the Blessed Virgin Mary, and I would never look back. I started praying the Rosary daily, instead of just carrying it around in my pocket and hanging it from my rearview mirror. And I started to recognize the power of asking the Blessed Mother for her intercession.

Mary stepped right into my world in a moment when everything felt like it was crashing down around me and held me in her loving embrace. It was undeniably an other-worldly experience.

It changed everything for me. In that moment, I realized the Blessed Mother was not just a character in two-thousand-year-old stories I'd been hearing for as long as I could remember. She is my mother. She is your mother. And she wants to have a relationship with *every single one of us*. She wants to protect us in times of pain, give us hope in times of difficulty, rejoice with us in times of happiness, and lead us ever closer to her Son so we can one day embrace her in heaven after a life well lived.

A seemingly infinite number of books have been written about the Blessed Virgin Mary. After all, as she predicted, *all* generations have called her blessed. Marian books approach her in various ways, from apologetic tomes to devotionals to Biblical exegesis related to her in both the Old and New Testaments. This book doesn't fall into any of those categories.

Instead, this book takes a moment to recognize the unique point in time in which we all find ourselves: the age of social media and bite-sized tweets, when we need to be able to defend and explain our relationship with Our Lady in 280 characters or less. This book is aimed at helping those of us who spend time posting about our love for Our Lord, our faith, and Our Lady across the various social media platforms, to help guide us in how to share that love in an effective manner that will lead our family, friends, and followers into a deeper appreciation for what we believe and why.

From developing our own relationship with Mary, to learning more about her, to defending her in mentions and notifications, this book is here to take you on a journey into her Immaculate Heart within the context of likes, retweets, and favs.

If you've ever wanted to learn more about Mary and grow in your relationship with her, let's go!

If you've ever wondered how to respond when Our Lady is getting attacked online, let's go!

If you've ever wanted to better understand how "retweeting her is retweeting Him," let's goooooo!

1
Staying On-Brand

Social media has changed *everything*. Like it or not, we have to accept that the internet, smartphones, and social media have absolutely changed communication and the world we live in forever. The old ways of communicating, sharing news and information, or keeping in touch with friends and family are falling by the wayside in favor of Facebook posts, Twitter retweets, and Instagram stories.

As usual, the Church has largely lagged behind as technology started changing. While the pope's English language Twitter account may have an impressive number of followers (18.2 million as I write this), he's still significantly lagging behind the likes of Katy Perry, Justin Bieber, and Barack Obama (each have more than one hundred million). As it usually is with technology and innovations in communication, the secular world got a jump start on the Church, and Catholics have been playing catch-up ever since. You can just have a look at the typical parish website if you don't believe me.

That being said, regular everyday Catholics like you and me are starting to recognize the need for us to adapt in order to continue to try and share the Gospel message with the world where the world is — and right now, that means especially in the world of social media. So, we are left with the task of reaching out to the world with the saving message of Jesus and His Church through the means of Facebook, Twitter, Instagram, and all the rest. The question is, how do we do this effectively?

Evangelization in the Age of Social Media

Social media is always changing, always on the move, always switching from one trend to the next. The meme that gets all the love on Tuesday will be seen as out-of-touch if someone tweets it on Friday. This sort of fast-paced communications environment means that to effectively engage with the world, we have to be paying attention to what's going on. While there's obviously a tremendous downside to always being logged on, there's also a lot of good that can come from checking your timeline a few times throughout the day.

The first is that social media gives us an opportunity to show that the Church is relevant. So many in our secular world, especially the often-talked-about "young people," look at our two-thousand-year-old hierarchical Church and assume that it has zero relevance to them or to the present world in general. We all have the opportunity to change that assumption by engaging with the world we find ourselves living in.

When we speak out on social media against injustice and link our speaking out to our Catholic Faith, it makes a difference. When we engage in discussions about politics that are engulfing our day-to-day interactions and lay out how our Faith compels us to stand on one side or the other, it gives people pause. When we can jump in on the latest meme that's got everyone laughing and put a Catholic spin on it, we insert our faith into the conversation while showing we can still have a good time.

Evangelizing in the age of social media is all about meeting people where they are and showing how the Faith is an important part of our daily lives, thoughts, and actions. It's about sharing the Good News in a way that can be consumed in bite-sized chunks. It's about being welcoming and showing the Church as a hospital for the sick rather than a hotel for the righteous. It's about having fun and engaging in a way that shows we're just a normal bunch of people who happen to love Jesus, Mary, and the Eucharist.

Mary?

That's right! Of all the misunderstood Catholic practices and teachings, our devotion to the Blessed Virgin Mary, Mother of God, reigns supreme. With social media giving everyone the platform to clear things up, doesn't it follow that we as Catholics should be using the means God has provided to share the Good

News about Mary? Many would say no and encourage the use of social media in the Christian world to focus on the things that bring us together, rather than the things that tend to split us apart.

But to that I say, "No way!" What I want to focus on is how to transform our social media use into something we can put out into the world for the glory of God. I want to lean into the

Share This! Does your parish have an awesome website, internet presence, or unique social media engagement strategy? Take a screenshot and share it on your favorite social media platform for all to see!

social media space with our Catholicism and spread the Good News of the Church founded by Christ. After all, we believe that the Catholic Faith has the fullness of truth, that it is the Faith handed down from Christ to His apostles, the Faith kept alive in the upper room after Jesus ascended into heaven, the faith Our Lady demonstrated as she calmed the anxieties of her Son's friends just before the descent of the Holy Spirit on Pentecost.

And we're not only looking to transform our social media use, we're looking to transform our relationship with Mary and through that transformation, to grow closer to her Son. Mary will always lead us closer to Jesus, and if we can get that message plastered on every screen around the globe, the love of Christ will pour into the world.

But First ...

It's worth noting that most of us have at times been less than charitable, snarky, or overly hyperbolic on social media for the sake of getting a rise out of people. If I can be brave enough to admit it to the world through this book, you can most definitely be brave enough to reflect on your social media posts and admit it to yourself as well. We Catholics have a long history of examining our conscience, after all, and in this world of retweets, shares, likes, and DMs, part of that examination has to include the reasons why we posted the things we did on social media.

Before we can talk about the Faith on social media, we need to honestly examine the ways in which we use social media now. And since this book is all about talking about Mary, defending Mary, and growing closer to Mary in our lives, I recommend that we start off by asking Mary to help us take an honest inventory of our presence and action on social media. Even if we use our platforms to share our faith, let's ask Mary to help us examine ourselves honestly. Are we posting content out of pride? Are we composing our posts with the intention of getting a rise out of a certain group of people? Are we purposefully obscuring the truth of the Faith just to make a joke?

I admit I've done all of the above, and I've even had to take some of my intentions in my social media use to confession. I continue to work to amend myself to be more authentic and charitable.

But it's hard.

I recognize my own pride just by way of clicking back on certain posts of mine to see how they've been received. Did that tweet get the likes and recognition I think it should have? Should I delete it if it wasn't popular? Should I retweet it myself just to get it more exposure? When I catch myself asking these questions about posts on social media, I know I need to step back and take a break. I have to work hard to constantly remind myself *why* I'm sharing the Catholic Faith on social media. If the spotlight is focused on me instead of the Faith, I've gone astray and need to reel it back in.

When it comes to sharing content aimed at making certain folks uncomfortable, ask Mary to help you remember that the people you interact with on social media, the people who read your tweets and like your Instagram posts, are *people*. It seems odd to say that, but when we're sitting down staring at a screen, we can tend to forget that our sisters and brothers are likewise sitting there staring at a screen. Our posts don't go into the void, as we sometimes joke about online; they're words that can build up or break down the Body of Christ. Posting on social media to get a rise out of certain groups certainly isn't building up.

Finally, let's ask Mary to help us avoid hyperbole, or over-stating something to make a point (or a joke, in my case). Do I purposely say things that stretch the truth for the purpose of getting some laughs? This has come up for me quite a bit with tweets I have shared. Making jokes about Catholics worshipping statues (we don't) or going way overboard in my word choices when talking about Mary (for the purpose of making non-Catholic Christians uncomfortable), are ways I've had to catch myself and recognize that I needed to work harder on remembering the reasons I'm on social media in the first place. It's important for us to remember that we're trying to share the truths of the Faith, and even when we make a joke, we should try to be clear and not confuse those who may not get the joke.

Checking ourselves before posting content is vitally import-ant in the social media world if we want to evangelize effectively and make sure we have our priorities straight whenever we log on.

Remember to Step Away and Pray

Head on into your phone's settings and have a glance at which apps are using up the most battery. If you are like me, you'll see your usage of social media far surpassing all the apps you have downloaded for prayer, biblical reading, or catechesis, and you'll need to take a moment to reflect and realize it might be time to *step away and pray*. One of the most valuable pieces of advice when it comes to sharing the Catholic Faith and our love of the Blessed Mother on social media is to take time away from your

Search This! Have you ever heard of the Twitter Litany of Humility from @teawithtolkein? Search on Twitter to check it out!

device. Take a break from the constant stream of notifications, be okay with missing out on the latest meme trending with your followers, and go back into the real world.

Leave the phone behind and go to your local parish to just sit in silent prayer. Close the laptop and head outside for a walk where you can reflect on the beauty of God's creation and just be in the present moment. Toss the tablet on the table and pick up some spiritual reading from the saints to immerse yourself in some timeless advice that you can use in all the various areas of your life.

A retreat from social media is necessary for getting our prior-ities back in order, for remembering that our focus needs to be on God and not on clicks. Believe it or not, your follower count isn't going to be the thing that gets you into heaven. It's going to be how much you loved God, how much you responded to His grace by loving your neighbor, and how much time you spent developing and improving your relationship with the Lord. Sure, we can take tiny steps in each of these areas on social media, but we can't make it the whole way. While it connects us with others in a certain sense, social media also separates us from our communities, keeps the real world in need at a distance, and can work against us if we aren't vigilant.

While it's important to reflect on the reasons we're engaging in social media, sometimes it's necessary to just step away. Even if we've perfected the art of posting content for the purposes of building up the Body of Christ and spreading the Good News, there still comes a time when we need to take a break.

I can't say it enough: *step away and pray.* And take the Blessed Mother with you. Once you've taken that much-needed time for yourself with Mary, come back and keep reading.

The Media Apostle's Playbook

We've all realized by now that social media has a lot of positives and a whole lot of negatives. We like to blame the social media platforms themselves for the negativity we experience, but if we're willing to be honest with ourselves, most of that blame falls on our shoulders.

The content we post, the replies we offer up, and the manner in which we curate who we're following goes a long way toward making our experience online either positive or negative. If we want to spread the Good News of Jesus Christ to the world through the means of social media, we've got to take time to reflect on what we're choosing to put out there *and* what we're choosing to consume.

When reflecting on the responsibility that comes with sharing the Catholic Faith on Facebook, Twitter, Instagram, and the rest, there is no one more suited to take us by the hand and guide us than the one and only Blessed James Alberione.

Born in the spring of 1884 in Fossano, Italy, young Giacomo Alberione was the fourth of six children in a family of farmers. A brief biography from the Vatican's archives explains that his call to dedicate his life to God came quite early: "When questioned by his first-grade teacher as to what he wanted to be when he grew up, he replied, 'I want to be a priest!'"

At the age of sixteen, he entered the seminary in Alma to do just that.

On New Year's Eve in the year 1900, on the cusp of a brand new century, James found himself kneeling before the Blessed Sacrament contemplating what the future would hold for Our Lord, His Church, and James's own life.

The Vatican details what happened next: "A 'particular light' seemed to come from the Host and roused in him a sense of obligation 'to do something for the Lord and for the people of the new century': he felt 'obliged to serve the Church' with the new instruments provided by human ingenuity.'"

This started Father Alberione down the path that eventually led to his founding of the Pauline Family, including the well-known Daughters of St. Paul, to help him carry out his mission to bring Christ and the Gospel to the world through the means of modern communication. He spent a great deal of effort making clear that he wanted the Pauline Family to be willing to engage in all forms of new media as they developed, almost prophetically knowing that technology would lead to developments in communication, and wanting to ensure the message of Christ and His Church would have a voice in that space.

Tweet This! Do you have a personal experience where you felt the presence of Mary as your mother in your life? Tweet it out!

Saint John Paul II called Blessed James Alberione the "First Apostle of the New Evangelization." I want to turn to Blessed James's own words and ask him to guide all of us through an examination of our presence and purpose on social media before we move forward together through this book:

> The word of St. Paul is always valuable regarding these thoughts: All that is true, just, pure, loving, revered, what is virtue and deserves praise, all this must be the subject of your thoughts.

Are all of my posts on social media focused on sharing things that are true, just, pure, loving, revered, virtuous, and deserving of praise?

As we engage in social media, our focus should be to keep the light of Christ alive and visible in that space. We aren't there to tear people down, snap back at others, or post negativity; we are there to build up the kingdom, draw people to the Church, and encourage non-Catholics to take a close look at what the Church and the sacraments have to offer.

> You are not related through natural kinship, but through a spiritual one, that which holds you together is neither by means of blood nor of the flesh, but the desire to serve the Lord together.

Do our connections on social media show evidence of the fact that we are all one body? When we see someone suffering on social media, do we pray for them and reach out to them? Do we offer to help those in need? Do we use social media as a means of speaking out against injustices around the world? Do we actually click on the Go Fund Me link and donate to those suffering, even if they're a world away?

Blessed James Alberione reminds us to stay focused on the fact that we are all sisters and brothers in the family of Christ, something that is so easily lost in our increasingly divided society. Father Alberione is calling us back to that family model of faith, and it's a message the world of social media so badly needs to hear.

> In the silence of the evening, during our examination of conscience, let us ask ourselves: Lord, are you happy with me today?

Do we ever look back over the content we've posted and ensure that our time on social media was spent in charity, compassion, and love? Put on the mind of Christ and ask, *Lord, are you happy with my posts today?*

It is important for us in all areas of our lives to make a serious examination of conscience at the end of each day, to see where we fell short, to thank God for His grace active in our lives, and to prepare to do better tomorrow. The same can be said for our time on social media. Rather than just scrolling through the endless stream of posts before we head off to bed, why not reflect on the content we put out and consider if God would be happy with the work we did in the digital vineyard that day?

DON'T Post This!
Seriously, take some time away from social media. Pray, place yourself in the presence of the Blessed Sacrament, ask the Holy Spirit to guide your social media use for the greater good of Christ and His Church.

Blessed James Alberione may not have lived during the age of social media we find ourselves in today, but the wisdom he gained through spreading the Gospel utilizing the media available to him in his own life is timeless, and more than worth our consideration today.

Before you push "tweet" today, take a moment to reflect on the words of Blessed James Alberione above and remember that you are a worker in the vineyard, a representative of Christ and His Church, even online. Let that thought guide us as we move forward together.

2
#Blessed

Developing and maintaining your
relationship with Our Lady

O ne of the first questions I ever came across after I started
sharing my love for the Catholic Faith and Our Lady on
social media was a pretty straightforward one: *Why do you need
to have a relationship with Mary?*

The simplest, most direct and true answer is: We need a relationship with Mary because she leads us into a relationship with
Jesus. She leads us closer to her Son and his Church, and that
should always be the goal of everything we think, say, and do.

To be absolutely honest, though, when I first received that
question, I'd never given it much thought. I mean, I just had a
relationship with her, but I never questioned why. As I pondered
this, I thought back to my days in high school, when that same
term "relationship" made me feel uncomfortable when connected
to my faith.

I grew up in Orange County, California, a self-absorbed land
where people are primarily focused on social status and which

high school parking lot is filled with the most luxury cars. There was one place, however, where the Christian Faith was openly discussed with vigor and a complete disregard for social boundaries: the Huntington Beach Pier.

For us high schoolers, this was the go-to destination on a weekend night. We would walk along the pier with nothing to do and just hang out. Every weekend, without fail, there would be an awkward interaction on the pier between ourselves and a Christian trying to get the word out about Christ and His offer of eternal life. Looking back, I see how cool it was that they were working for the Lord out in public, but at the time few things made me feel more uncomfortable than a stranger walking up to me and asking about my "relationship with Jesus."

Hop on Facebook! Share your thoughts on having a relationship with Christ. Does it come naturally for you? Has Mary helped you with this relationship?

The idea of having a relationship with Jesus was very foreign to me. That's not to say I didn't have such a relationship; I mean, what could be more intimate than receiving Our Lord in the Eucharist? It's just that, as a Catholic, I didn't speak the same language as the Christians approaching me on the pier weekend after weekend.

As a quick aside, I still remember this one time when I was so fed up with being approached and asked this question that I randomly walked up to a bearded biker-looking dude on the pier and role-played for the fun of it.

"Do you have a relationship with Jesus?" I asked, with my friends looking on from afar.

"Do I?" the man responded, and then proceeded to unbutton his collared shirt, revealing a T-shirt emblazoned with an image of the crucifixion accompanied by the phrase "Paid in Full."

My cheeks turned red, and I scurried off, embarrassed, only to have my friends tease me about it for the rest of my life.

Back to this question at hand, though, lobbed at us by well-meaning non-Catholic Christians: *Why Mary?*

We have to realize that for non-Catholics, our devotion to Mary doesn't make a whole lot of sense. After all, 1 Timothy 2:5 says, "For there is one God, and there is one mediator between God and men, the man Christ Jesus." (I'll bet you didn't expect Bible verses to be hidden in a very Catholic book, did you? Well, I'm happy to surprise you!)

That seems like a pretty clear passage. Thanks to the Incarnation, Passion, and Resurrection, we have been brought into a close relationship with God Himself through Our Lord and Savior Jesus Christ. He's ready, willing, and waiting to hear our prayers and answer us in our needs. Why on earth would we spend our time developing a relationship with anyone else?

The *very* simple answer is: *Because Jesus wants us to have a relationship with Mary.*

Let's walk through exactly what that means.

Mary, the Proto-Christian

Our Christian brothers and sisters love to ask: Have you accepted Jesus into your heart as your personal Lord and Savior? These same Christians, who are hesitant about having a relationship with Mary, might be surprised to realize which human being accepted Jesus as Lord and Savior before anyone else.

Spoiler alert: It was Mary.

Our relationship with Mary starts by looking to her as a model, an example for what it means to accept Christ as Savior and jump headfirst into a relationship with Him. She accepted Jesus even when doing so didn't quite make sense. She accepted Jesus even though the circumstances made it difficult. She accepted Jesus knowing full well that He would be a sign of contradiction and that she would suffer as a result of doing so.

We look to her, we develop a relationship with her, as our guide in the Faith. She shows us what it means to give up everything for Him, to live a life radically altered forever after an encounter with Jesus. When life becomes a struggle, when we feel confused or overwhelmed by our circumstances, when we feel lost or ostracized, we can take solace in knowing that Mary understands what we're going through. When we turn to her, we see what the answer is: "Do whatever He tells you."

The story of Jesus' first public miracle at the wedding feast at Cana provides a really important framework for answering the question "Why Mary?" It's a well-known story for obvious reasons, but it can be easy to overlook the role of Mary, as the emphasis is placed on the amazing miracle Jesus performed. (Mary wouldn't want it any other way, by the way.)

Mary finds out that the wine has run low, and she immediately takes action. She walks up to her Son and says, "They have no wine." It's so simple, so quick. She recognizes who He is and knows that He will know exactly what she's saying. Jesus responds, "O woman, what have you to do with me? My hour has not yet come." While this may sound kind of like an insult tossed at Mary, we know this can't be the case. Jesus lived out the Ten Commandments perfectly, including "honor thy father and mother," so there must be something deeper going on in this interaction.

In fact, it would seem that Jesus is calling Mary "woman" as a way of connecting her to "the woman" from way back in Genesis 3:15, where God says to the serpent: "I will put enmity between you and the woman, and between your seed and her seed; he shall bruise your head, and you shall bruise his heel." Rather than talking down to His mother, Jesus seems to be trying to tip us off to the fact that His mother is the woman foretold as a key part of our salvation after our first parents fell.

As if to confirm this idea, Mary doesn't get upset when Jesus calls her "woman." Instead, she gives the servants instructions that are meant for every single one of us: "Do whatever he tells you" (Jn 2:5). In these five short words, Mary gives us the key to how we should live our lives.

And as if that wasn't enough, this story of the wedding feast at Cana shows us exactly what happens when Mary intercedes. They need wine, Mary tells Jesus they need wine, and Jesus performs a miracle in direct response to His mother's intercession. This isn't just a nice story about Jesus' first miracle, and it isn't just a story about how Jesus can do incredible things; it's also a story about how Mary's intercession is powerful, and how *if it is in line with God's will*, Jesus will do *anything* Mary asks of Him. And guess what? Because she's full of grace and free from original sin, she wouldn't even consider asking Him to do something that wasn't in line with His will. Her will is perfectly conformed to His.

So why Mary? She's the absolute perfect and most powerful advocate on our behalf. If the prayer of a righteous person is very powerful, as the Bible says (see James 5:16), there's nobody I'd rather have approaching the throne of God for me than Our Lady.

Okay, So Now What?

Now that we've looked at *why* we should have a relationship with Mary, we need to consider the question of "How?" Once we begin to see the powerful role of the Blessed Virgin Mary in salvation history and our personal lives in particular, *how* do we go about developing and maintaining relationship with her?

There are innumerable saints down through the ages who provide a blueprint for kicking off devotion to Mary. From Saint Dominic handing down the Rosary, to Saint Louis de Montfort developing and spreading the Total Consecration to Jesus through Mary, to Saint Maximillian Kolbe's style of total consecration. Before we get to those, however, I'd like to focus in on the very simple idea of Mary being our mother.

Yes, she's the Mother of God, the Word made flesh on earth. But, she's also *our* mother in a very real and profound sense. Her role as our mother was assumed at the foot of the cross, where she stood beside Our Lord and Saint John the Evangelist. As Jesus neared death, he used the last bits of his energy and life force to utter some very important words, conveyed through the Gospel of Saint John: "When Jesus saw his mother, and the disciple whom he loved standing near, he said to his mother, 'Woman, behold, your son!' Then he said to the disciple, 'Behold, your mother!' And from that hour the disciple took her to his own home" (Jn 19:26–27).

In his Gospel, Saint John often refers to himself as "the disciple whom [Jesus] loved." He uses this title as a tool to help us place ourselves in the story at moments when a crucial message or important point is meant for all of us down throughout history. The scene at the foot of the cross is one of those moments. There are a couple of things happening here. First, Our Lord is placing His mother under the care of one of His best friends, entrusting John with the task of guarding Mary throughout the remainder of her earthly life. Jesus is also pointing out to all of us the profound truth that Mary is our mother and we are her children.

This was a life-changing revelation for me, especially after the death of my own mother.

Why is this important to answer the question of "how" we develop a relationship with Mary? Because Mary's motherly role in our individual lives is the source of our devotion and relationship. The more we see her as our mother, the more our devotion can flow from there. If you're a visual person, the best place to start is to consider Mary's mantle. Head on over to your favorite search engine and plug that phrase in right now. The icon of Mary's mantle gives us a strong visual image of her role and her care for each of us as individuals.

Mary wants to protect us, she wants to take care of us, but even more so, she wants to walk with us through this valley of tears. This last part was the key for me to develop and maintain my own relationship with Mary. As I first began to develop a relationship with her, I saw her exclusively as the pinnacle of God's creation, an untouchable, perfect human, the model for all of us by her conforming of her will to that of her Creator.

She *is* all of that, of course, don't get me wrong, but the thing that really sparked my relationship with Mary was that in spite of all that, she also lived a life of deep suffering and unimaginable pain. She was not spared because she was sinless. She was not spared because of the special role she was asked to play.

Post This! Mary's love language is quality time. What's your love language and how can you incorporate that into your relationship with Mary and her Son?

This hit me hard at a time when I was going through my own darkest night, ten years after the death of my mother, now facing the impending death of my fourth son due to birth defects, feeling sorry for myself, and wondering why God would allow such terrible things to happen to those He loves, who try their best to love Him back. Mary crept into my thoughts, and I suddenly realized: Here we have the Mother of God, the person who had the most intimate relationship with Jesus of anyone who ever walked the earth, yet God allowed her to suffer.

Despite Mary being the crown of creation, despite her being the one through whom all graces would flow, despite her being the spouse of the Holy Spirit, the mother of the Word made flesh, and the most beloved child of the Father, *God allowed her to suffer.* It can sound trivial if we just pass over this thought quickly.

After all, God allows all of us to suffer. Yet when we allow ourselves to contemplate the idea further, we see precisely just how profound it is. She was not spared from sorrow, suffering, or even the death of her beloved Son. Instead, she was told from His earliest days that "a sword will pierce through your own soul also, that thoughts out of many hearts may be revealed" (Lk 2:35).

Mary, the one whom all generations would call blessed (see Luke 1:48) suffered just like you and me.

This is what made Mary "click" for me and made her reachable in a very powerful sense. I was now able to see myself in relation to her, able to see how much closer she was to me than ever before, and I was finally able to allow her into my heart as my mother in the midst of my sorrow.

Keeping It Up

Just like a good relationship with someone here on earth, our relationship with Mary needs to be maintained, worked on, and developed over time. So, the next obvious question is: How do we maintain a relationship with the Blessed Virgin Mary once we've begun it? We can't just text her and ask if she'd like to grab coffee after Mass on Sunday. How can we keep going forward in our walk with her to ensure that we don't just let this relationship wither up and die?

The key to maintaining our relationship with Our Lady is surprisingly similar to the ways in which we maintain relationships with our good friends here on earth — those friends who build us up and push us to become a better person. The keys are conversation, vulnerability, and prioritizing quality time.

Have You Called Your Mother Lately?

"Have you called your mother lately" has been a popular meme on Catholic social media for some time, a little joke for encouraging people to pick up their rosary and reach out to Mary. This is a good thing in many ways, as the Rosary is a great devotion for growing closer to Mary and thus walking with her to grow closer to Jesus. The problem is the Rosary — like many rote (or memorized) prayers — can easily become just another box to check: Pray the Rosary on my morning commute (check!). Pray mid-day prayer around lunch time (check again!). Pray the Divine Mercy chaplet on my commute home from work (check!) Pat self on the back!

I've learned that I need to take a moment to pause this routine and see if it's really accomplishing the goal God has in mind for me. Prayer is obviously good. Prayer is never wasted. But, if the purpose of my prayer is simply to check a box and then feel good about myself for having a consistent prayer life, I think I'm missing the point. And this is true of the Rosary as well.

Snap This! Take a picture of your favorite go-to rosary and post it to Instagram or Facebook with one of those lovely filters. Ask people to reply with pics of their favorite beads.

If I'm not careful, I could pray the Rosary every day and still not be doing anything for my relationship with the Blessed Mother and thus not growing closer to her Son. This is where the idea of having a conversation to maintain a relationship with Mary comes in. Beyond rote prayers, I need to take the time to converse with her, sharing my pits and peaks from the day and asking for her protection and help in certain areas of my life. Only then can I start to grow in a way that really helps me remember how much I rely on her, how much I rely on Christ, and how much both of them love me.

The hard part is that this style of prayer doesn't seem to come easy for us cradle Catholics. Many of us have been brought up to see spontaneous, conversational prayer as distinctly Protestant.

As we grow in our faith and try to foster a serious and authentic spirituality, we have to make some serious effort to move our prayer life in this direction.

The big step forward for me, as I mentioned before, was embracing the role Mary has in my life as my mother. Once I started to envision her as my mother, I realized I could converse with her, and my prayer life flourished. Recognizing her role allowed me to spend my commute to work just talking with her, sharing my dark trials, expressing my joy and thanksgiving for the blessings God has given my family, and seeking her help and guidance. Sure, I still prayed the Rosary while making the nightmarish Bay Area commute (it's a *really* long commute), but I approached it in a radically different way. I went from checking off the boxes to seeing it more as connecting with her as a person who cares about me, cares about my life, and wants to know about what's troubling me.

Post This! Got a favorite icon of the Blessed Virgin Mary? Post it to Instagram!

Let Mary Make You Uncomfortable

For better or for worse, the one thing that turns an acquaintance into a friend is vulnerability.

I'm sorry. It's true.

If conversations with "friends" go no deeper than the weather, the current political news, or the price of gas, the relationship isn't going to be a very meaningful one. For a friendship to grow and develop, there has to be a deeper level of sharing, an experience of opening ourselves up and letting another person in.

This is *much* easier said than done. Many of us, myself included, like to keep our private life private and our deepest inmost selves even more so. At the same time, we have a yearning to connect with others, a pull toward giving and receiving love in community, and this requires allowing ourselves to be vulnerable, even (to some extent) on social media. In my own personal social media use, I've found quite a lot of support when I've opened myself up. Not that we should be airing everything about ourselves and our lives on social media — far from it. But reaching out to our circle of social media friends and followers and pulling the curtain back on our struggles, our coping strategies, and everything in between can open us up to the love that comes with community. And that can be a beautiful thing.

The same goes for our relationship with the Blessed Virgin Mary. If we want to develop and maintain a relationship with her, we've got to work to let her into the most intimate and hidden parts of our lives. In my life, that included welcoming Mary into the darkest moment I had ever experienced shortly after finding out we were expecting our fourth son.

Overwhelmed at first, since we had three kids five and under already running around the house, we slowly settled into a sense of excitement about what God had in store for us this time around. That sense of excitement shattered in a single moment about halfway through the pregnancy. At the typically exciting ultrasound appointment where you find out your baby's gender and go home with photos only a parent could love, we were instead handed news that would change our lives forever.

The ultrasound uncovered a lack of fluid in my wife's womb, which eventually led to a diagnosis of renal agenesis. Our brand new baby, our fourth son, a child we already had big plans and big dreams for, whom we had already fallen deeply in love with, was handed a death sentence.

To say we were devastated would be an absolute understatement.

The anger that I felt toward God at the death of my mother paled in comparison to the blinding rage I felt at the death of my son. I still remember the first Mass we attended after getting the news. I walked to the back of the church with our fussy one-year-old and stood before a stained-glass window of Jesus with children all around him, one even sitting on his lap. I stood before that window and raged at the Lord silently in my head. How dare He! How dare He give us the gift of this child, only to rip him from our arms so suddenly, so needlessly.

I lost the will to pray. I lost the desire to be close to God. I lost hope.

While my wife and I walked through this journey together, at the same time it felt so very lonely. Not many people can understand the pain of losing a child. Not many people can imagine what it's like to be at a hospital while your wife gives birth to a beautiful baby, only to hold him in your arms as he dies just an hour later. Not many people understand the despair, the hopelessness, and the grief that comes with such an intense experience.

As I struggled to pray through the remainder of the pregnancy, knowing full well that my time with my son was growing shorter by the minute, I pulled out my rosary. I wasn't expecting anything at all, but I felt like it was all I could do. I didn't have it in my heart to reach out to God in conversation, despite the fact that I wanted to come to Him in tears begging for help. But I *could* recite the Rosary, even if it was nothing more than words at this point.

As I prayed the Rosary on my way to work one day, it hit me. Similar to the experience at my mother's funeral when peace and joy flooded over me, I had an unexpected realization that would change my perspective. Up until now, I had felt like God had abandoned my wife and me, leaving us to suffer without relief.

Now I realized that I wasn't alone.

I realized that the Blessed Virgin Mary knew my pain in a deeply personal way.

Mary knew this very pain. Mary understood what it felt like to hold a dying son in her arms.

Mary understood the struggle of giving herself over to the will of God despite wishing it could happen any other way.

Mary understood me.

While this realization and comfort didn't change the outcome of our situation, it brought me a sense of peace and relief that could only be attributed to Mary actually stepping in to walk alongside me. Once again, Mary embraced me and comforted me in one of my darkest moments.

Quality Time Is Mary's Love Language

Every so often, my wife and I have the same realization: We are in serious need of a date night! Even if it's just chips and guacamole after (finally) tucking the kids into bed, even if it's just promising to sit on the couch and share our days with each other before collapsing into bed ourselves, we recognize we *need* quality time with each other if we want to feel connected. This usually comes after three or four days of consistently streaming Netflix and staring at our phones after the kids go to bed, and crashing into a realization that we haven't been connecting the way we need to.

That one night of connection and quality time helps us to remember just how important it is to set everything aside for our relationship, and while we fall victim to binging streaming videos again and again, we always return to the same conclusion. The busier our lives become, the more we need to block out time for things like prayer, playing with the kids, and yes, even eating chips and guac with each other.

In the same way (you guessed it), we need quality time with Mary if we want to develop and maintain a good relationship with her and as a result grow into a deeper relationship with Christ. If we don't set aside quality time for our spouse, kids, family, and friends, our relationships will suffer. If we don't take the initiative to set aside quality time to spend with our Blessed Mother, our relationship with her isn't going to go anywhere, and we close ourselves off to her attempts to carry us deeper into the heart of her Son.

For me, this all goes back to developing a routine. Whenever I have down time, I inevitably drift into some form of entertainment. When I find myself with nothing to do in a given moment, I typically pick up my phone, rather than my rosary beads, and this is why setting a routine has become so vital for me to set aside quality time with Our Lady.

I have to schedule time to be with her. This means setting aside routine and scheduling times for praying the Rosary, praying the Little Office of the Blessed Virgin, reading about Our Lady in writings of the saints or other authors (which you're totally doing right now, so, score!), or setting up time to just sit and talk with her about everything I'm going through. It's all about setting the time aside, even if you find it difficult.

Share This! How have you grown in your relationship with Mary? Was it through a saint with a strong devotion? Was it through a specific prayer?

Why is it so important to make time to spend with Mary? Because Mary will lead us to Jesus. This is her core mission. This is the end goal of our relationship with her. Jesus listens to the prayers of His mother, who is constantly interceding on behalf of her children. So we had best make time to be close to her, the one who wants nothing more than for us to be close to Him.

3

TIL (today I learned)

What the Church teaches about the Blessed Virgin Mary and why

On the feast of the Assumption a few years back, I posted a very simple and respectful tweet of appreciation for Mary: "Happy Feast of The Assumption!" I'm sure, if you've ever public-ly shared on social media about your devotion to Our Lady, you know what happened next. My mentions got lit up pretty quickly.

"You Catholics worship Mary."

"Catholics believe Mary is the fourth person of the Trinity."

"Jesus called Mary 'woman' and that *proves* He didn't think she was important."

These comments go on and on, especially in the world of Twitter, where user identities can be less personal than on other platforms. While the big misconceptions about Mary are pretty easy to spot and dispel, there are others that can leave even the most sure-of-themselves Catholics unsure how to respond. Per-haps you've been faced with questions that left you wondering, *Do we believe that? It does seem like we offer her quite a bit of devotion — is that okay?*

It's important, therefore, to take a look at what the Church actually teaches about Mary, not only so we can clarify and educate those who have misconceptions, but also so we can help keep ourselves on the right path when it comes to properly honoring the Mother of God. Later in this book, we will delve more deeply into ways we can defend Marian teachings in the brief format of social media. But first, we're going to stack up the building blocks to our defenses of common responses to the Marian dogmas.

Immaculately Conceived

The Immaculate Conception is quite possibly the most misunderstood Marian dogma. It is certainly the clear winner when it comes to Catholic clarification posts on social media. If I had a dollar for every time I saw a tweet that read "Happy Feast of the Immaculate Conception, which is about the conception of Mary, *not* Jesus btw" … well, let's just say I would find it harder to enter the kingdom of heaven than a camel squeezing through the eye of a needle.

While the mix-up between the Immaculate Conception and the Incarnation is the most talked about misunderstanding when it comes to this Marian teaching, it isn't the most substantial one that you need to know about.

Let's start with what the Immaculate Conception actually means.

According to paragraphs 490 and 491 of *The Catechism of the Catholic Church*:

> To become the mother of the Savior, Mary "was enriched by God with gifts appropriate to such a role." The angel Gabriel at the moment of the annunciation salutes her as "full of grace." In fact, in order for Mary to be able to give the free as-

sent of her faith to the announcement of her vocation, it was necessary that she be wholly borne
by God's grace.

Through the centuries the Church has become ever more aware
that Mary, "full of grace" through God, was redeemed from the
moment of her conception. That is what the dogma of the Immaculate Conception confesses, as Pope Pius IX proclaimed in
1854:

> The most Blessed Virgin Mary was, from the
> first moment of her conception, by a singular
> grace and privilege of almighty God and by vir-
> tue of the merits of Jesus Christ, Savior of the
> human race, preserved immune from all stain
> of original sin.

Catholics believe that God saw it fitting for the mother of His son
to be sinless, filled with grace from the moment of her conception. Can you imagine a more beautiful way for the one through
whom the Savior of mankind would enter the world to be created?

Unfortunately, the beauty and wonder of this incredible truth
is not clear to many believers. This may be due to misunderstandings about the teaching, or to certain ideas that are taught in other faith traditions, particularly non-Catholic traditions.

The first criticism of the Immaculate Conception (as with
most Marian dogmas) is that it isn't found anywhere in Scripture. Before responding to this criticism, Catholics must realize
a couple of things: First, it *is* true that many of the understand-
ings we have about Mary are not explicitly noted in Scripture.
Second, the Bible never teaches that everything we believe as
Christians must be found in Scripture. This needs to be the first
starting point of any discussion questioning any Catholic teach-

ing on the grounds of Scripture.

Getting past that, while Scripture does not outright teach that Mary was immaculately conceived, there are definitely passages that back up the teaching.

The first such passage actually cracks me up. Some detractors believe that Jesus calling Mary "woman" at the wedding feast at Cana (Jn 2) indicates that she's not important. Actually, this passage points us to the foreshadowing of the Immaculate Conception hidden in Scripture, all the way back in Genesis 3:15. God says, "I will put enmity between you and the woman, and between your seed and her seed; he shall bruise your head, and you shall bruise his heel."

In this passage, God is talking to the serpent after Adam and his beloved wife eat the fruit of the Tree of Knowledge of Good and Evil. God tells the serpent, the evil one, "I will put enmity between you and the woman, and between your seed and her seed."

Post This! The Immaculate Conception is the national patron of the United States. Share your favorite image of the Immaculate Conception for all to see!

First question: Who is this woman God is referring to? The answer comes in the second part of the statement: " ... between your seed and *her* seed." It sure does seem odd that God would mention *her* seed, unless He was talking about a woman who would conceive a child *without* the seed of a man.

Okay, we're getting closer.

Next, God said He would put *enmity* between the evil one and the woman he's referring to. At its most basic, the word enmity means *the state or feeling of being actively opposed or hostile to someone or something.* Some other words for enmity can also help, such as hostility, antipathy, aversion, hate, and loathing. The woman referenced by God in this passage way back at the beginning of our human story, the one who would come and bear a child without the seed of a man, would be completely immune to the attacks of the evil one, the one through whom all sins enter the world. He would not be able to touch her.

To top it all off, we return to that often misunderstood moment when Jesus calls Mary "woman." Since we know Jesus practiced the commandments with absolute perfection, and we know those commandments include "honor your father and mother," we have to conclude He wasn't calling her "woman" as an insult.

So what was He doing?

He was pointing us to a very important detail about His mother: *She* is the woman referenced in Genesis 3:15. She is the woman who would have enmity placed between her and the evil one, between her and sin, and *her Son* would be the one to crush the head of the serpent all those years later on the cross.

Let's take a quick breather ... that was pretty intense.

The other main issue non-Catholics have with the Immaculate Conception is that they assume if Mary was saved before Jesus died on the cross for all of our sins, it must follow that she didn't need a Savior, and that would fly in the face of everything we know about the necessity of Jesus' death and resurrection in atonement for our sins.

They're right! That *would* fly in the face of Jesus being the Savior of all mankind, *if* that's what the Immaculate Conception meant. But it doesn't.

We can walk through a brief exercise on common sense to help clarify this one. The sacrifice of Jesus on the cross opened up the opportunity for salvation to all, both those who lived at the time of Christ and those who lived before and those who would come after. Because God is outside of time, not bound by it as we are, the saving power of the cross can work backward and forward through time.

Most of us agree that those who lived lives adhering to the grace of God before the time of Jesus were able to receive salvation after his death and resurrection. So it makes sense that Mary needed Jesus as her Savior just as all of us do — He just applied the merits of His cross to her beforehand. His work on the cross allowed Mary to be free from sin from the moment of her conception and throughout her life. Without her Savior, none of that would have been possible.

When you think about who Jesus is, it really only makes sense that His mother would have needed to be a worthy vessel to bring Him into the world for all of us. Sometimes God figures out ways to do things that just absolutely blow our minds and surpass anything we could have come up with; and that's the case here.

And it's wonderful.

Perpetual Virginity

"Therefore I ask Blessed Mary ever-Virgin, all the Angels and Saints, and you, my brothers and sisters, to pray for me to the Lord our God."

Catholics around the world pray this prayer at Mass, mentioning the perpetual virginity of Mary. In the same breath, we ask God to forgive us our sins, and we ask everyone else to pray for God to be merciful with us. It's a beautiful reminder of our sinfulness, our absolute dependence on God's mercy, *and* Mary's virginity. She was a virgin at the time of Our Lord's conception, remained a virgin during Our Lord's birth, and maintained her virginity throughout the remainder of her life.

Many Christians find this reality of Mary puzzling, especially in light of our current cultural context, which finds virginity in *any* situation to be bizarre. Why would Mary and Joseph have needed to remain chaste throughout their marriage? Doesn't the Bible clearly state that Jesus had brothers and sisters? In the sixth chapter of Mark, we read: "'Is not this the carpenter, the son of

Mary and brother of James and Joses and Judas and Simon, and are not his sisters here with us?' And they took offense at him" (Mk 6:3).

There are actually two possible explanations for this reference to Jesus' brothers and sisters, and I'll touch on them briefly — though I'm not a Scripture scholar by any stretch.

The word used for brother in Greek (*adelphos*) described not only biological brothers, but also more distant relatives (cousins, for example), and even "spiritual brothers." A great example of this would be Saint Paul's writing in 1 Corinthians 15:6, where he recounts: "[Jesus] appeared to more than five hundred brethren at one time."

Tweet This! Post on Twitter (or your favorite social media platform) about Saint Joseph. Encourage your followers to grow in their devotion to Saint Joseph, protector of the Holy Family.

That same word, *adelphos*, is used in this context, and even those most opposed to the perpetual virginity of Mary wouldn't be so bold as to suggest Mary had over five hundred children, right?

If that explanation of the brothers of the Lord doesn't satisfy, I would turn next to a document known as *The Protoevangelium of James*. This document, which presents itself as being composed by Saint James sometime in the second century, talks about the life of Mary prior to the Gospels. While this document is not scriptural, it is widely seen as a reliable source of historical information.

This document describes Saint Joseph as an older widower with children from his previous marriage, who was selected to be the husband of Mary because he would be able to protect her and maintain a chaste life, since she had consecrated herself to the Lord as a virgin. If this is truly what happened, it could follow that those brothers and sisters of the Lord mentioned in the Gospel could also be Jesus' step-siblings — children of Joseph, but not children of Mary.

All that being said, many are sure to persist in their opinion that Mary was only a virgin up until the birth of Christ and then went about her business as a typical married woman (we could have a whole conversation about that word "until" and how its biblical connotations are different than ours today, but we'll hold off for now).

Here's the problem: If Mary did not remain a virgin, it throws the entire virgin birth into question. We believe that Mary conceived Jesus by the Holy Spirit, and part of the evidence for this claim is the fact that Mary remained a virgin. When the angel appeared to her at the Annunciation, she asked, "How can this be, since I have no husband?" (cf. Lk 1:34). The implication is that, even though she was betrothed to Joseph, she did not intend to stop being a virgin after her marriage. If she did go about business as usual in the marriage department after the birth of Jesus, any skeptic would be well within their right to ask: Well, if she had babies the normal way *after* Christ, who's to say that Jesus wasn't born the normal way as well?

Her perpetual virginity sets her apart, and it is right and just that our Blessed Mother would have consecrated herself in this way, as a spouse of the Holy Spirit, remaining dedicated to God and His plan for her above and beyond everything else.

Divine Motherhood

"How can you say Mary is the Mother of God? God is eternal! Are you trying to say Mary is eternal too?"

This actual response from an actual conversation I had with an acquaintance about Mary really blew my mind. I couldn't come up with an intelligent response. All I could manage to say was, "Um ... Jesus is God ... Mary is Jesus' mother ... so Mary is

God's mother." As you can guess, that argument didn't convince my friend.

When you're brought up understanding something, it can often be difficult to put it into words. You know what you believe, you know it's true, and yet it can be challenging to share that belief (and the reasons for that belief) with others. For me, this is especially true of the teaching that Mary is the Mother of God.

It can be helpful to approach this teaching by examining what the Church means when she calls Mary the Mother of God. The Catechism states: "Called in the Gospels 'the mother of Jesus,' Mary is acclaimed by Elizabeth, at the prompting of the Spirit and even before the birth of her son, as 'the mother of my Lord.' In fact, the One whom she conceived as man by the Holy Spirit, who truly became her Son according to the flesh, was none other than the Father's eternal Son, the second person of the Holy Trinity. Hence the Church confesses that Mary is truly 'Mother of God' (*Theotokos*)" (495).

Search This! Look up icons of the *Theotokos* and post your favorite one to Instagram. Maybe include a prayer to Mary, Mother of God.

The Catechism breaks it down more succinctly in paragraph 509: "Mary is truly 'Mother of God' since she is the mother of the eternal Son of God made man, who is God himself."

This teaching of Mary as *Theotokos* (literally "God-bearer" in Greek) is often misunderstood to mean that Mary is somehow the source of God's divinity. This obviously cannot be true, since Mary is a creature who has not existed for all eternity. She came into the world two thousand years ago and was a human being who walked the earth. She is not divine herself, so she can't be the source of anyone else's divinity. But she is the Mother of God because she carried in her womb the divine person of Jesus Christ.

Jesus Christ is God.

Some thinkers in the Church's history tried to work their way around this by claiming that Mary was the mother of Jesus' human nature, but not the mother of His divine nature. Yet mothers don't give birth to natures; they give birth to persons. Mary conceived, carried, and gave birth to a person, and that person has two natures: the nature of God and the nature of man. Because Jesus has a divine nature, Mary is indeed *Theotokos*.

And don't just take my word for it. From the earliest days of the Church, saints and scholars have understood this fact about the Blessed Virgin. One of the Fathers of the Church, Saint Irenaeus, in his work *Against Heresies* from the year 189, wrote: "The Virgin Mary, being obedient to his word, received from an angel the glad tidings that she would bear God." In AD 431, this was settled once and for all with the Council of Ephesus, assigning the title *Theotokos* to Mary and declaring it to be true.

Assumption

Every August 15, we Catholics come up with a plan for a quick dinner, then rush out the door (with kids possibly in pajamas) to make it to Mass on time (or shortly thereafter). We do this in honor of the Solemnity of the Assumption of the Blessed Virgin Mary. But what are we actually celebrating?

Paragraph 966 of the Catechism is here to help us out: "'Finally the Immaculate Virgin, preserved free from all stain of original sin, when the course of her earthly life was finished, was taken up body and soul into heavenly glory, and exalted by the Lord as Queen over all things, so that she might be the more fully conformed to her Son, the Lord of lords and conqueror of sin and death.' The Assumption of the Blessed Virgin is a singular participation in her Son's Resurrection and an anticipation of the resurrection of other Christians."

The Catholic Church holds that, at the completion of her

earthly life, Mary was taken up body and soul into heaven in anticipation of the resurrection promised to all of us at the end of the world. (We can debate later if Mary actually underwent bodily death. The Church has left this question open.) While this understanding of Mary's assumption was held from the earliest times of the Church, it wasn't until 1950 when Pope Pius XII made an infallible statement, in the Apostolic Constitution *Munificentissimus Deus*, officially defining the dogma of the Assumption.

Non-Catholic Christians point out that this dogma is most definitely not mentioned in Scripture, but Catholics have a couple of places they look to for evidence to support the claim. Revelation 12:1–5 is perhaps the most obvious:

> And a great sign appeared in heaven, a woman clothed with the sun, with the moon under her feet, and on her head a crown of twelve stars; she was with child and she cried out in her pangs of birth, in anguish for delivery. And another sign appeared in heaven; behold, a great red dragon, with seven heads and ten horns, and seven diadems upon his heads. His tail swept down a third of the stars of heaven, and cast them to the earth. And the dragon stood before the woman who was about to bear a child, that he might devour her child when she brought it forth; she brought forth a male child, one who is to rule all the nations with a rod of iron, but her child was caught up to God and to his throne.

This vision of Saint John in the final book of Scripture is surely talking about the Blessed Virgin Mary, appearing crowned and coming from heaven, which would seem to support the Catholic teaching that she's reigning from there.

Another idea that has always helped to convince me of the truth of the Church's teaching on the Assumption is that Jesus is the New Adam and Mary is the New Eve. Saint Paul references Jesus as the New Adam (cf. Rom 5:12–21 and 1 Cor 15:45), and it is only fitting that the New Adam should have a New Eve by his side in his work. Mary, as "the woman," undid the damage done by Eve, and God's grace flowed into the world from her *fiat*. Way back in Genesis, when Adam was kicked out of the Garden as a punishment for not following the will of God, there is no mention of Eve leaving the Garden with him. However, we all know that she did, because they had children, populated the earth, and continued on with their lives (cf. Gn 3:22–4:26).

Share This! Hop on Facebook and post about other saints who were carried up into heaven to show that the Assumption is most definitely not ruled out by the Bible. Google it, read about them, and start posting!

If Eve followed Adam out of the Garden, despite it not being explicitly mentioned in Scripture, wouldn't it make sense that the New Eve would follow the New Adam, even if Scripture was likewise silent? Instead of following him out of the Garden, however, this time she would be following Him body and soul into heaven.

It's beautiful to think of Mary, the crown of creation, being assumed through God's power up into heaven as a sign of her importance, rather than undergoing bodily corruption as the rest of us do after death. And for me, it greatly aids my ability to have a personal relationship with Mary, knowing she's up there, fully alive, looking down on me and smiling.

What This Means about Mary

There are several other teachings and beliefs about Mary's role in the Church that flow from these four dogmas. Some of these are worth exploring before we move on. While not infallibly defined, these other teachings about the Blessed Virgin Mary are generally accepted as true within the Catholic Church. Granted, bringing them up in conversations with those who question Mary's role in salvation history may prove counterproductive, it's still important to know what they are and why they are reasonable. If nothing else, these teachings can help us cultivate our own relationship with Our Lady!

Mary as Advocate
As the spiritual mother of all people, Mary is our personal advocate before the throne of Jesus, interceding on our behalf for all our needs. Reflecting back to the earlier section on Mary at the wedding feast at Cana, we can plainly see the role she had while on earth. She walked up to her son and told him simply, "They have no wine," which led to Jesus taking action. She continues to have that role for all of us now in heaven. She is our advocate, and thanks be to God we have her as such!

Mary as Mediatrix
The great Saint John Vianney plainly called Mary the mediatrix of all graces when he said: "All the saints have a great devotion to Our Lady: no grace comes from heaven without passing through her hands. We cannot go into a house without speaking to the doorkeeper. Well, the Holy Virgin is the doorkeeper of heaven."

Grace comes to us through Jesus, to be sure, but it was through Mary that God chose to bring Jesus to the world, and thus it would follow that all the grace from Jesus went through her hands and came into the world as a result of her *fiat*.

Mary as Co-redemptrix
As we've shown so far in this chapter, Mary has a pretty serious

role in salvation history. And, since the Redeemer of the world came through Mary, it makes sense to consider her the co-redeemer, as it were. This title in no way diminishes the saving work of Jesus, of course, as Mary's role would mean nothing without Him, but it sheds light on the profound mission of Mary as the one through whom the Redeemer came.

Learning about the Church's actual teaching on the Blessed Virgin Mary, her role in salvation history, and her role in our lives personally is absolutely essential for developing and maintaining a relationship with her. It's also critical for being able to defend her, both in real life and on social media. We can't have a relationship with someone unless we know them, learn about them, and take a genuine interest in what they're all about. And we most certainly can't stand up for someone and defend their honor unless we work to understand what the truth is about them so we can guide misunderstandings back toward that truth.

Post This! Take a moment to consider how the intercession of Mary at the wedding at Cana sheds light on the power of her intercessory prayer for us in this present moment. Share your experiences and thoughts with your followers.

And, boy, there are certainly some misunderstandings about the Catholic Church's devotion to Mary! But, to be fair, if we take a step outside and look at ourselves, the reasons for the confusion may become more apparent, and that can help us better understand where those who disagree are coming from.

4

No Filter

Recognizing how Marian devotion looks from
the outside and clearing up the confusion

R efreshing my mentions on Twitter on the feast of the Immaculate Conception one year, I came across one that said (and I
paraphrase), "You keep worshiping Mary and see where that gets
you!"

As a lifelong Catholic who understands the difference between *latria* (the supreme worship due to God alone) and *hyperdulia* (the special veneration due to the Blessed Virgin Mary), I
responded in the typical way: "We don't worship Mary! Whatever
gave you that idea?" Feeling good about doing my due diligence
to clear up misinformation about our faith, I then went to Mass
(it was a holy day of obligation, remember?) where we venerated
the Blessed Virgin Mary on her special day. A statue of Mary was
processed in and prominently placed near the altar. Every single
hymn that day was about Mary and her wonderful role in salvation history. And after everything was said and done, we joined
together in singing the *Salve Regina*, a hymn in which we honor

Mary as our life, our sweetness, and our hope.

Okay, okay, so maybe it's not *so* strange that Christians looking at the Church from the outside develop misconceptions around our devotion to Mary. I mean, to be fair to them, we do kneel before statues of Mary, pray to her, consider her the Queen of heaven and earth, have *lots* of special days specifically set aside to honor her, and even talk about our total consecration to Jesus through her. And, to be fair, there may be some Catholics out there who allow their veneration of Mary to cross a line and move beyond hyperdulia. In general, however, most Catholics understand what Saint Maximillian Kolbe taught: "Never be afraid of loving the Blessed Virgin too much. You can never love her more than Jesus did."

The point worth pondering is that our conversations with non-Catholic Christians about Mary may go more smoothly and be more productive if we can manage to take our Catholic glasses off for a bit and consider what our devotion to the Mother of God might look like to those on the outside. That way, we can respond with, "Yes, I see how you came to that conclusion," and then follow with, "Let me explain what was going on and what we actually believe to help give context to what you're seeing and hearing."

We have a tremendous opportunity living in the age of social media, and with that comes a great responsibility. We have to work to find that sweet spot of sharing the truths of the Faith, sharing the truth about the Blessed Virgin Mary, while at the same time being willing to accept how it might look to others. And it falls on all our Facebook posts, tweets, and Instagram Live videos to be that bold embrace of those angles for the rest of the world to see.

Praying to Mary

On a weekend morning shortly after we had our first child, I was working in the front yard when two Jehovah's Witnesses walked up my driveway with big smiles on their faces. Recently reverted to the Faith and obsessively listening to Catholic Answers Live at the time, I had a big smile on my face, too. I leaned my broom up against my car, crackled my knuckles, and pulled all of my best recently learned responses to their common challenges to the forefront of my mind.

As it turned out, one of the members of this JW tag team was a former Catholic, who claimed to have left the Church over his view that the Church was taking money from the faithful at every Mass for the sole purpose of amassing ridiculous amounts of wealth. I found that to be an odd assertion and wondered if he'd ever actually glanced at the inside of the collection basket as it went around. But I rolled with it and engaged in a fairly peaceful discussion with them.

They trotted out their typical points and arguments in favor of their view of the world,

Post This! What's your favorite apparition of Mary? Look into the actual words she spoke during that apparition and post them on Facebook to inspire your friends and followers today.

and I snapped back with questions about the Real Presence of Christ in the Eucharist and the clear biblical indication that Jesus founded a Church and left His Holy Spirit with that Church to help guide us through complicated issues of faith and morals. We hit an inevitable impasse, and as we wrapped up our conversation and the pair started their way down my driveway, I let my pride and arrogance get the best of me and exclaimed to the fallen-away Catholic, "I'll pray for you … to Mary!"

I felt pretty haughty and full of myself at that point. Looking back, I realize I allowed myself to miss out on an opportunity to be a humble witness; instead I said something I thought would really grind their gears. But the point remains, most non-Catholic Christians (and yes, even Jehovah's Witnesses) just don't understand why we pray to Mary.

What Does "Pray" Even Mean?

At the root of other Christians' disapproval of Catholic prayer to saints (and especially Mary) seems to be a disconnect in the way we use the term "pray." In the conversations I've had, I have realized that for non-Catholic Christians prayer is typically relegated to adoration, worship, and other things solely set aside for God Himself. Coming from this angle, it makes sense that they find it bizarre that Catholics pray to anyone except God.

So, before we go on with apologetic arguments, it might be worth it to make sure everyone is on the same page with the terminology.

When Catholics use the word "pray," we mean two different things: First, we mean prayer of worship and adoration directly aimed at God alone; second, we mean asking individuals (Mary and the saints, for the purposes of our conversation at the present moment) to pray for us. I find this distinction at the onset of a conversation on this topic to be extremely helpful, as it kicks things off by dispelling the misconception that we are giving to others something that should only be directed at God. Only then can we move into an argument about why we should ask the saints in heaven (and our friends here on earth) to pray for us.

Share This! What's your favorite Marian feast day and why? Celebrate the day by hopping on social media to share what makes it your fav!

The Rosary

So maybe your explanation can help your non-Catholic friend understand that we aren't praying to Mary in the same way we pray to God, but they might still wonder, *What's the deal with the Rosary?* Once again, I think it's important to take a step back and see how the Rosary looks from the outside looking in. It's a repetitive prayer focused on Mary! Didn't Jesus condemn repetitious prayer, babbling on with many words? "And in praying do not heap up empty phrases as the Gentiles do; for they think that they will be heard for their many words" (Mt 6:7). Besides, you could be spending that time praying to Jesus Himself, rather than focusing on Mary.

The answer might surprise you as much as it surprises them. The Rosary is actually a meditation on the Gospels! That's right, as we thumb through those beads and recite prayers many of us have known since before we could read, we're actually focusing our mind on different stories of Jesus' life. From beginning to end, we're filling our hearts and minds with the life of Christ (His life on earth and His continued work in and through the Church) and engaging in what is actually known to be the highest form of prayer: contemplation.

As for Jesus' supposed condemnation of repetitious prayer and heaping on of words in the Gospel of Matthew, it helps to read through the passage a little more carefully. Jesus condemns meaningless repetition and *empty* words, but the prayers we repeat during the Rosary are anything but meaningless, the words we meditate with are anything but empty. In fact, we're repeating the Our Father (the prayer Jesus taught us) and the Hail Mary, which is the words of the angel Gabriel and Elizabeth to Mary as recorded in Scripture.

Two final points about the Rosary: First, Catholics have to remember to guard against using the Rosary in a superstitious way, as if praying it "just right" means we'll get whatever we want. First and foremost, the Rosary is a meditation on the life of Christ. In addition, it is an extremely powerful prayer for bringing our intentions to Christ through the Blessed Virgin Mary. But whenever we pray the Rosary for a specific intention, we need to remember: "Thy will be done."

Next, we must not view the Rosary as a requirement for Catholics. The Catholic Church contains an immense treasury of prayer and spiritual practices, and each of us will find that some resonate with us and others don't. When we find specific prayers that are meaningful for us and help us draw closer to Our Lord, great! If that happens to be the Rosary, great again! However, not everyone connects with the Rosary, and we shouldn't be pushing it as something people have to do, a sort of box you have to check if you want to call yourself Catholic.

Statues of Mary

Walk into any Catholic church, and you will almost certainly be greeted by an assortment of statues — statues of saints, angels, Jesus … and statues of Mary have pride of place, of course. Many of our Protestant brethren question this practice, and we need to be able to take off our Catholic lenses in order to understand their concerns about our veneration of these representations of heroes from days past.

After all, Catholics kneel before statues and kiss statues and leave flowers and other tokens of admiration in front of statues. It makes sense that non-Catholics would assume that we're praying to those statues, or even that we might believe certain statues are deities or possessed with magical powers. I don't know about you, but I've had to jump into my mentions on social media with an all caps response like this: "FOR THE LAST TIME, WE DON'T WORSHIP STATUES!"

It's probably more effective to have a clear understanding up front, and then to lay the groundwork whenever this conversation comes up. I have found there are a couple of good ways to start this conversation and get it going in the right direction. First off, clear out any misconceptions that we believe the statue is the person or being we are praying to. Believe it or not, there are folks out there who actually think we're praying to the statue. After clearing that up, point to the idea of having family pictures around the house. There aren't very many people who would find it weird that I have a picture of my deceased mother up in my home, and sometimes I look at her picture and say something along the lines of, "Help me with these kids, Mom!"

The photo of my mother is a reminder of her presence in my life, a reminder that I'm still connected to her even though she's gone from this life. The statues, holy cards, and images we have around our churches and our homes of the Blessed Mother, Jesus Himself, or the saints, are beautiful reminders of the fact that we are connected to them in an intimate way as members of the Body of Christ. They are also a great reminder of our call to be holy as they were.

Visions of Mary

Stepping it up a bit from the issue of statues, Catholics also believe in Marian apparitions — events here on earth where the Blessed Virgin Mary appeared to a seer or seers and left a message meant for the whole world. (We'll touch on these in more depth in chapter 9.) The Church has approved only a small number of these reported apparitions, and Catholics are not required to believe in them, since they constitute private revelation. Still, most Catholics are deeply devoted to specific apparitions of Mary, and in America some of our favorites are Our Lady of Guadalupe (this image is practically everywhere in America, from images hanging in our churches to T-shirts to fleece blankets), Our Lady of Lourdes, and Our Lady of Fátima.

Snap This! Do you have a favorite statue of Mary around the house or at your parish? Share a photo of it for all of us to see!

In trying to share the Church's teaching on Marian apparitions with our Christian sisters and brothers, there are a couple of starting points that I have found quite helpful. First, as mentioned above, Catholics are not obligated to believe in, subscribe to, or have devotion to any of the Marian apparitions. The Church doesn't force the faithful to believe that the Blessed Virgin Mary has appeared to anyone. Now I do want to point out that there is plenty of evidence that Mary most certainly has appeared to certain people (miracles, conversions, prophetic messages, etc.), but we still aren't obligated to believe in the various approved apparitions.

Next, remember that Mary does not appear to people on earth through her own power or plan. Whenever Mary has appeared on earth, it has only been made possible through the power and will of God Himself. He is the one in charge, He is the one who appoints a time and place for the Blessed Mother to appear, and she appears only to proclaim His Gospel message and the urgency of heeding that message. Mary gives no new revelation in the approved apparitions, she provides no new instructions, and she offers no other path to salvation than the Cross.

Putting these guard rails up on Marian apparitions can help quell concerns. Only after laying them out can you help people begin to understand just how cool it is that Mom stopped by to say hi!

Feast Days of Mary

Packing up my things and getting ready to head home a bit earlier than usual one day, I had a co-worker ask me where I was going. "Today's the Solemnity of the Immaculate Conception of Mary, so I'm heading out early to get a good seat at Mass!" We stared at each other in a brief awkward silence that seemed to last a very long time. I finally broke the silence with, "Well, see you tomorrow!"

It can be hard to explain to non-Catholics why we would go

to Mass in the middle of the week to celebrate the Blessed Virgin Mary. (Feast days that don't include an obligation to attend Mass are another matter altogether.) Once again, we take a step back to consider where we should start in our explanation to help ensure we are clearing up the common misconceptions surrounding our devotions to the Mother of God. First off, yes, we go to Mass to worship the one true God. But Mass is a time where we come together to join in prayers of adoration, contrition, petition, and thanksgiving with the whole Church (and this includes the faithful on earth, the saints in heaven, and the souls in purgatory!). The Church asks us to come to Mass on certain Marian feast days to thank God for the role He gave the Blessed Virgin Mary in salvation history; to thank Jesus for giving His mother to us in His final moments on the cross; and to thank God for the role He allows Mary to continue to play in our daily lives.

Tweet This! Have you ever wished you could replay a meeting with non-Catholic missionaries who came knocking at your door? Tweet your perfect (charitable) response!

When we attend Mass on Marian feast days, we're looking toward God in wonder and awe at the way He decided to have Mary come into our lives as our example, advocate, and mother. Mary always points us to Our Lord. As she put it at the wedding feast at Cana, "Do whatever He tells you" (Jn 2:5). This is her role in our lives, to remind us to follow Jesus without reservation, without holding anything back. Her feast days remind us of that advice, and as we reflect on her role in our world, our Church, and our personal lives, it's the advice she continues to pass down to us throughout history. It's the key to eternal life, the key to a joyful life on earth, and the key message she wants us to hear.

The three Marian feasts (solemnities) when the Church asks

the faithful to attend Mass in the United States are the Assumption (August 15); the Immaculate Conception (December 8); and Mary, the Mother of God (January 1). On each of these feasts, we're recognizing the incredible plan of God down throughout the ages and thanking Him for the fruits of that plan. Much like the moon reflects the light of the sun and produces absolutely no light of its own, Mary reflects the love of Christ, His salvation, and His light to us. Without Christ, Mary can do nothing (just like the rest of us), but she was perfectly compliant with His will and His plan for her life, and as we recognize this, we actually become more focused on Him than anything else.

The Way We Talk about Mary

Each of us has the ability to clear up the misconceptions many have about Mary to help move everyone closer to loving her as we do. That being said, the way we talk about Our Lady can lead to misunderstandings about our relationship with her.

Catholics use some pretty elevated language to describe the Blessed Virgin Mary, and we have to recognize this fact when we discuss her with our non-Catholic friends, and especially when we post about her on social media. We also need to make sure that our language isn't drifting away from Church teaching and into murky waters. Often, the way we speak about Mary, even in prayer, can make it seem like Mary has power in and of herself. We know Mary isn't divine, but when non-Catholics hear us asking her to directly intervene in our lives, they can misunderstand what we mean.

When we pray to Mary, what we mean is *Mary, please go to Jesus and ask Him to help me with this situation.* But it can sound like *Mary, help me with this situation.* So for instance, if I pray, "Mary, heal my mother from this terrible illness," I'm not actually capturing the entire truth of our Church's teaching with my words. It's a short-hand version of what I mean, which is that I want Mary to ask Jesus to heal my mother. Those on the outside looking in may not understand what we understand.

But the way we speak about Mary is nothing compared to what the saints have said about her. Consider Saint Louis de Montfort, who authored *True Devotion to Mary* and started the Total Consecration to Jesus Through Mary, a spirituality and devotion that I have found great comfort in. Those Catholics who totally consecrate themselves to the Blessed Virgin Mary actually consider themselves her *slaves* and slaves of Jesus *through* Mary.

Imagine telling your non-Catholic coworkers about that! But Saint Louis de Montfort doesn't hold back when it comes to Mary. Consider this quote from his book *True Devotion to Mary*: "When Mary has struck her roots in a soul, she produces there marvels of grace, which she alone can produce, because she alone is the fruitful Virgin who never has had, and never will have, her equal in purity and in fruitfulness." This is just one of many examples I could pull from *True Devotion*. Even a

Update This! Have you completed the Consecration to Jesus through Mary? If so, why not update your bio with "Slave of love of Jesus through Mary"? It'll be a conversation starter.

good Catholic might read this and wonder if it is an acceptable way to speak about Our Lady. It is! But I think there's a little finessing that needs to be done to help understand why.

First: "She produces there marvels of grace, which she alone can produce." When De Montfort makes reference to the grace Mary "alone" can produce, he's speaking of her ability to produce these graces *through* Christ. All grace comes from Christ, but it comes to us through Mary, the one who mediated the grace of Christ to the world through her *fiat*. One of my favorite things about our Catholic Faith is the understanding we have of how

God works through men and women here on earth to impart His grace and His love to us. We see this in the prayers of a friend helping us through a difficult time; the homily of a priest turning us back toward God with renewed vigor; the unconditional and self-sacrificial love of a mother toward her child showing us the love God has for each one of us. When Saint Louis de Montfort says Mary "produces marvels of grace, which she alone can produce," he most certainly means that she alone can produce those graces *through* God, *through* Christ.

Next, the author says of Mary that she "never has had, and never will have, her equal in purity and fruitfulness." What about her Son, you know, Jesus? De Montfort knew that Mary is not equal to, or surpassing in, the purity and fruitfulness of Christ. Instead, he is using hyperbole to prove his point that Mary is the crown of creation, the highest of all created beings, the one who is full of grace. He's not suggesting in any way that she ranks above the God-Man.

That being said, Mary holds a very special place in salvation history. While we should go out of our way to help other Christians understand what we mean when we use elevated language about the Blessed Virgin, we also have to be careful to not undervalue the role she plays in salvation history and more personally in all of our lives. While she is a creature with nothing of value apart from Christ, she is at the same time the crown of creation, the highest created being ever to exist. We do not need to be ashamed of the hyperdulia due to Mary, and we should not hide from it, even when others question us. Instead, we need to do all we can to help them understand Mary's role — and offer the invitation for them to begin to honor her, too!

5

Defending Mary in the Mentions

Responding to common attacks on Mary
in 280 characters or less — with charity

So why should we share about Mary on social media? This isn't a new question in the realm of evangelization, but rather one that has to be revisited again and again. Why should we talk about Mary at all? The argument might go: When we're evangelizing the culture, shouldn't we stick to the stuff that binds us together rather than the topics that tear us apart? In other words, shouldn't we stick to the less obviously religious topics when evangelizing the secular culture? Helping the poor, standing up for social justice, the need to protect the environment, etc. And similarly, when evangelizing our Christian sisters and brothers, shouldn't we stick to the topics we agree on, like Jesus dying for us, our dedication to following Him, and the excitement of looking forward to heaven?

The theory is that we connect with others through our commonalities, and once they've bought in a little bit, we can start to share the reasons why we believe certain things they may not believe.

As I jumped into social media back in 2014, I realized one thing for sure: This tactic didn't work for me. When I logged into Twitter and cracked my knuckles before typing out some Catholic content, I felt compelled to lean in even further with my Catholicism. I preferred to share precisely the things that separated us from our non-Catholic Christian sisters and brothers, not because I wanted to be divisive (at least, I don't think I did, but more on that later in this chapter), but because I wanted to let my Catholicism hang out as much as possible and then provide clarifications for those who didn't understand or took issue with it.

Rather than trying to bring people into the fold by sticking to our commonalities until right before the baptismal water hit their heads, I preferred to start with the hard stuff, start with the tricky topics that most people wanted to avoid. Starting with the topics that divided, it seemed to me, was the way to spark interest online and get people talking. Less than being about getting clicks for the sake of clicks, it was more about getting content spread around, hoping that the more people saw it, the more they would be curious about Catholicism and be compelled to look into it.

What I'm getting at with this is that it's *so* important to share about the Blessed Virgin Mary, precisely because of the role she wants to play in the life of every single person. She's ready to intercede, protect, and walk with you and with me, and people need to know that. How is devotion to the Blessed Mother ever going to increase in our world if we don't talk about her? How are people going to grow into a relationship with Our Lady if we aren't tweeting about her? How is anyone going to know about the incredible message Mary has shared with the world through her apparitions if we don't post beautiful images of Juan Diego's tilma — cloak — on Instagram?

We are missionaries. We are compelled by way of our baptism and confirmation to go out into the world and spread the Catholic Faith. That means the Good News of Jesus, which includes the role of the Blessed Virgin Mary. As Catholics, it is our job to evangelize about Our Lady precisely because Mary helps lead people to Jesus. And the internet and social media have given us an opportunity to spread that message beyond our small communities and local range of influence.

Social media is for staying connected with family, of course. It's a great way to engage in fun and have a good laugh, sure. But we cannot pass up the opportunity to utilize social media as a means of sharing (and continuing to learn about) our faith. We need to get online and talk about

Post This! Have you ever been able to pull yourself away, rather than get sucked into a negative back-and-forth on social media? Share a post about how that felt.

Jesus, Mary, the Eucharist, confession, and the saints. We are called in this present time to be missionaries in the digital world for the sake of saving souls, guiding understanding of our beliefs, and promoting exactly how the Church remains relevant in our modern culture.

So, pick up your phone and tweet about Mary *right now* …

Typical Replies to Marian Content and How to Handle Them

But be prepared! If you start sharing about the Blessed Virgin Mary on Facebook, Twitter, Instagram, or any other platform, your replies are going to start getting busy. Even something as innocent as "Happy Feast of Assumption of Mary" has the potential to fill your mentions up with strangers questioning why you are tweeting about "non-biblical nonsense." Let's take a moment to look through a few tweets I have put out myself, and some of the comments they received.

When I picked up my phone and shared that Mary was "the Queen of Heaven and Earth, our life, our sweetness, and our hope" (from the Salve Regina), I quickly received a very typical response condemning Catholics for idolatry. For those who may not know, idolatry literally means the worship of an idol, and it is most definitely condemned early on in Sacred Scripture: "You shall not make for yourself a graven image, or any likeness of anything that is in heaven above, or that is in the earth beneath, or that is in the water under the earth; you shall not bow down to them or serve them" (Ex 20:4–5).

Search This! Search for your favorite Marian meme of all time and share it. Encourage your friends and followers to reply with their favorites.

Obviously, as a Catholic, I say, "Amen!" Worship is reserved for God alone, and as we addressed in an earlier chapter, Catholics do not worship Mary. This is why it's worth making sure you're prepared, because this will most definitely be one of the items you find when you head back onto social media and check your notifications after sharing your love of Mary. In short, the best way to respond to this is to agree that idolatry is absolutely wrong and to gently and succinctly point out that idolatry is not what's going on when it comes to Catholics and their devotion to Mary.

Next up was a nice little tweet I sent out that read: "The Pope infallibly declaring Mary as Mediatrix and Co-Redemptrix would be a perfect way to celebrate Reformation Day, in my humble opinion." I can be humble enough to admit there was a wee bit of snark in this tweet, but in my defense, have you seen the kind of stuff being tweeted by our non-Catholic Christian sisters and brothers on Reformation Day? Someone had to do something! Granted, I could have finessed that tweet a little more, but the response I received was one that you're going to find quite often if you start sharing about Mary on social media: What about 1 Timothy 2:5? "For there is one God, and there is one mediator between God and men, the man Christ Jesus."

In other words, how can we call Mary a mediator for mankind when the Bible so clearly shows that Jesus is the only one? This response is an extremely common reply to tweets about the powerful intercession of Our Lady. The most pithy and effective way to answer this complaint is to point out that we are all mediators between God and man. Whenever someone asks us to pray for them, and we take their intentions to the Lord, we are acting as a mediator. You would be hard-pressed to find any Christian who doesn't believe in praying for others. In fact, that same letter to Timothy explicitly instructs us to do so. Showing the similarities between what we do for one another and what Mary does for each of us can go a long way toward clearing things up. Of course, Jesus is the one mediator, but we are all mediators *through* Him.

Finally, I'll take you to a time I shared this tweet: "How do I know Mary's intercession is powerful? I know because just touching the rosary beads in my pocket brings me peace and consolation. I know because praying the Rosary feels like an out-of-this-world experience. I know because Jesus showed it to be true." Within seconds, my phone buzzed and alerted me to the fact that what I was claiming was nowhere to be found in Scripture.

This is perhaps the most common reply to posts about the Blessed Virgin Mary. We face this argument often, thanks in part to the stereotype that Catholics don't know their Scripture. There is a certain sad truth to that stereotype, but thankfully there is a solution: Read the Bible. If you're not in the habit, start small by going through the daily Mass readings on your phone and moving up from there.

Even if you don't read the Bible as much as you should, it's important to remember that not everything we believe is contained in Scripture. Hit that reply button and type: "Where in the Bible does it say everything we believe has to be explicitly mentioned in the Bible?" It may seem somewhat silly, but this has to be the starting point to answer this accusation, every time. It asks the person stepping into your mentions to show where their argument comes from, thus knocking them off of their game by putting the burden of proof squarely in their lap. And, spoiler alert, the Bible *doesn't* say what they think it says.

Sure, 2 Timothy 3:16–17 says: "All Scripture is inspired by God and profitable for teaching, for reproof, for correction, and for training in righteousness, that the man of God may be complete, equipped for every good work."

Amen! But this passage doesn't say Scripture is *sufficient.* Saint Paul doesn't say it's the *sole* rule of faith, and anyone who claims that's what he meant is reading something into Scripture that isn't explicitly mentioned.

One fairly common response to this line of argument is, "I gave you a Scripture reference, and I'm still waiting for you to give me one." Touché. Still, it's an important place to start because many of our non-Catholic Christian sisters and brothers haven't been challenged on this point before. It can at least plant a seed for more contemplation on the matter.

Oh, and by the way, there are plenty of scriptural references noting the power of Mary's intercession, once you make it to that point in the conversation. From the wedding feast at Cana (John 2:1–11) to the teaching in James 5:16 that "The prayer of a righteous man has great power in its effects" (after all, has there ever been a created being as righteous as the Blessed Virgin Mary?), our belief in the power of Mary's intercession is firmly rooted in the sacred texts.

Getting the Point Across in 280 Characters or Less

In late 2017 Twitter doubled the character count limit for tweets from 140 to 280, and its users were aghast. It seemed as though the entire reason for Twitter's existence, the format that all had become so accustomed to, was being completely flipped on its head. In full disclosure, when the change was first made, I would immediately scroll past tweets that made use of the updated character limit. It just didn't look right.

I can look back on that point as the moment when I realized exactly what social media had done to my attention span. Can you imagine 280 characters feeling like too much information to absorb in a single sitting? Don't even ask what happened to me when I tried to read more than a few pages in an actual book. (Remember books?)

Tweet This! Find a meme of a current Twitter trend, and put a Marian spin on it. Then toss it out for all to see!

While Twitter isn't the preferred social platform for everyone, I offer this as an example of the way social media has shaped our consumption of information. Everything, from breaking news to philosophical debates to jokes, has undergone a transformation. Everything has to be broken down into bite-sized chunks lest people just scroll right past it without so much as a glance. This means when it comes to evangelization in social media apps, we have to adapt to getting the point across in the most pithy way possible as well.

In all fairness, you have every right to see this as a negative development in our culture. The depths of the truths of the Faith are unfathomable, after all, and it takes a bookshelf filled with tomes to even scratch the surface of the Church's many teachings. But perhaps there's another angle to take. Perhaps the increasing importance of getting the point across without fluff is going to help the Church reach more of those who are searching.

When you only have 280 characters to share something you believe and why you believe it, you have no choice but to get to the point. You've got to leave all the flowery language behind and give people the goods as efficiently as possible. If content that is short and to the point is the best way to connect with our peers in the present communications climate, then that's exactly how we're going to give it to them.

If you're posting about the Assumption, say what the Assumption is and why it means something to you in your current life. Sure, there's so much more you could say, so much praise you could heap on God for this lovely event in salvation history, but let's get to the point so people can see why the Assumption is powerful and why it applies to us now.

Using the Language of Our Time

One important way to get the point across in tweet-sized chunks and make sure people are going to be able to hear what you're talking about is to post and share using the language of our times. And I don't mean simply using terms and vocabulary that will make sense to those engaging in social media (although that's vitally important as well). I mean utilizing the current means of transmitting communication via social media as a way of making sure we're present in the current conversation.

This means taking the popular meme floating around the internet that week and updating it to reflect a Catholic truth or spinning the latest joke format and importing something about Mary into it. It means opening ourselves up to sharing live video, creating a thread of our friends singing a hymn, pushing out podcasts that share the Faith (even if we don't like the sound of our voice!). When we utilize the trending jokes, memes, and content to transmit Catholic ideas, it opens up our reach beyond our tiny Catholic corner of the internet.

Taking over a meme and "baptizing" it may be one of the most effective ways of getting our Catholic content out there, and it allows people to consume it without feeling threatened, without feeling like they're being preached at. Instead, it allows them to laugh along at a joke as they scroll on their phones, and perhaps plants a little seed they might not even realize is being planted because they're focused on the humor.

Slipping in the evangelization without anyone knowing — that's the good stuff.

Share This! Have you ever had a difficult interaction about your faith on social media that went well and ended positively? Share it so others can see that it's actually possible!

Enter: The Trolls

Before you step into social media to share your love of the Blessed Virgin Mary, please be aware: You will be welcoming the trolls into your mentions. For those who haven't ventured into these waters before, a troll is someone who antagonizes others online by deliberately posting inflammatory, irrelevant, or offensive comments or other disruptive content. As you can guess, the trolls start coming out in force when you start sharing about Our Lady.

Typically, these interactions manifest as quick, cutting, outright hateful comments directed at Mary and Catholics in general. They aren't the start of a genuine conversation where two sides can learn something through the interaction, but instead are meant to do nothing more than boil one's blood. The troll is out to push you over the edge and goad you into a reaction full of anger, frustration, or trolling back.

Resist this urge. Or, to utilize the language of our time (since I mentioned that above): DO NOT FEED THE TROLLS. If you refresh your notifications and find a handful of folks replying in a manner that really gets you going, don't reply. Don't give them the satisfaction. After all, they're hoping to get at you, make you frustrated, lead you to act in a way that is less than charitable to them. Keep scrolling. Don't give in.

Trust me, you'll feel better after ignoring their replies.

Interested in a Real Discussion?

Sometimes, however, there are folks who are interested in a real discussion, and figuring out who those folks are and who they are not can be a real art form. It can get even more complicated by the fact that at first glance, they may look identical. "Where is that in the Bible?" may be an actual invitation into a discussion with someone who is sincerely interested in learning more about why we believe something they can't seem to find in Scripture. When you point out chapter and verse that gives a nod to the teaching about Mary, you may get a reply along the lines of, "That's interesting. How does that line up with … " and you're on to the next step in the conversation. These can be great discussions on social media and can actually help both sides to learn something.

For Catholics, social media gives us a great opportunity to practice defending our faith with charity and kindness in a manner that can be heard. In addition, we get to see where our non-Catholic Christian sisters and brothers go in conversations like this, and it can help us to better approach the topic with others in the future. It can also give us some food for reflection on our own beliefs, while encouraging us to go back and learn more.

We also have to be reflective enough on the conversation to see when it isn't headed anywhere, when it's just a matter of someone wanting to air all of their negative grievances against the Church, and step away. Not before, however, mustering all the courage and charity God's grace can give us to reply with, "I'll pray for you. God bless." I know you'd rather say something negative instead, but trust me, kindness is good for the soul.

Know When to Walk Away

Both the positive and negative experiences noted above circle back to a very important skill we all need when it comes to our conversations on social media: knowing when it's time to continue a conversation and when it's time to wrap it up. Even when someone engages with us in an authentic manner interested in getting at the truth, there still may be a time to call it quits or at least to call timeout. One can really only get so far on social media, and we have to be able to admit that it's not the ideal medium for engaging in a conversation that could get fairly deep fairly quickly.

We have to realize when we're just going to have to call it off and agree to disagree. I've experienced this quite a bit. For instance, I get the question "Where is that in the Bible?" and respond with the question "Where does the Bible say everything we believe has to be found in the Bible?" As we've noted before, the most predictable response is 2 Timothy 3:16–17, and also as we've noted before, my response is to point out that this verse doesn't actually say what my friend thinks it says.

Search This! Search for your favorite Marian meme of all time and share it. Encourage your friends and followers to reply with their favorites.

At this point, I can get a sense for whether the conversation should continue or if I need to call it quits. I can sense it's good to continue if the response is something like "I see your point. I'll have to think about this more." That response shows a genuine understanding of the situation and interest in getting to the truth. But if the response is more like "I gave you a verse from Scripture, now you have to give me a verse," then it's probably best to consider the conversation closed, and to move on in charity.

Knowing when to continue the conversation and when to

call it quits can go a long way toward helping you maintain your sanity while interacting online. This may seem like a silly thing to say, but it's true! Conversations where you're trying your best to be charitable and informative in response to questions can be absolutely maddening when the responses are negative and often seemingly unrelated. It doesn't take long to get sucked down a rabbit hole of pointless conversation that leaves you feeling flustered and needing a drink.

Don't let it happen! Put the phone down and walk away! There's no obligation to continue on with someone online just to try and prove your point or win an argument. You can simply scroll through your mentions and ignore replies whenever you want.

6

That Feel When ...

How sharing our relationship with Mary might
do more convincing than apologetics

"**F**aith has nothing to do with feelings!"
It's likely that you've heard this response more than once
when engaging in a conversation about faith. Be it online or in person, some folks want to separate faith from feelings, and they try to
shut down any conversations that seem to rely too much on feelings.
They argue that feelings are fleeting, they come and they go, and
the truth is the truth no matter how you feel about it. Okay, sure, at
a very stripped-down and basic level, this assertion is correct. Even
when we *feel* like God isn't hearing our prayers, He is. Even when
it *feels* like those committing evil in the world get by without any
consequences, they don't. Even when it *feels* like God doesn't love us,
doesn't care if we're suffering, He does.

And yet, there is something very real about our feelings,
something deep, something that has a huge impact on our faith
journey independent of the fact that our feelings don't determine
truth. Feelings impact our relationship with God, and they have

an effect on our spirituality, our prayer life, and our ability to commit to pushing harder to become the saints God created us to be.

Feelings matter.

As Catholics, we are a both/and people, not an either/or people. We can hold that two truths about feelings co-exist and do not cancel each other out. On the one hand, faith has nothing to do with feelings. The existence of God and all the truths revealed to us through Scripture and the Church continue to be true no matter how we feel about them. At the same time, our feelings have a huge impact on our faith journey, our desire for holiness, and our closeness to God and His plan for us.

Tweet This! Why does Mary matter in your life, right here and right now? Share a tweet about the impact she has had in your life and your walk with Jesus!

The interesting twist that I have found in my personal life is this: The times that my feelings suggested I was deserted by God, left to suffer without reason and without relief, those moments when I felt most covered by the darkness of life, least able to pray, and most alone in my pain, in retrospect, were the exact times when I was drawing closer to God than ever before.

When we enter into the deeps of sorrow and suffering, Jesus is there. When we feel like everything is going wrong in our lives even though we are striving for holiness like never before, Jesus is there. When we look up to the heavens in anguish and heartache and call out, "My God, my God, why have you forsaken me?" Jesus is most definitely there. There's something mysterious about suffering, from hurt feelings to our soul being absolutely crushed, and while our feelings may lead us to struggle with our faith for a time, God is right there, holding us close, willing to wait it out until we are able to see the bigger picture.

As I touched on earlier in the book, the death of our sweet little son, Luke, less than an hour after we welcomed him into this world, absolutely crushed me. Even though we knew his prognosis in advance, there was simply no adequate amount of preparation for that moment when he came and left in such a brief period of time. His birth was a moment of unconditional love and joy that is still difficult for me to explain, since it was in the midst of tragedy and heartbreak, but in the days and weeks that followed that moment of love and joy, depression, hopelessness, and anger rose to the surface.

How could a loving God allow such evil, pain, and suffering in the world? How could a God who cares about us allow one of us to die so near the beginning of life? How could God permit such pain into my family's life even when we were trying our hardest to grow closer to Him?

These seemingly impossible questions kept swirling in my heart and soul as I tried and failed to pray in the days following our son's death. Instead of silently repeating, "Jesus, I trust in you," I more often found myself repeating, "How could you?" through a deluge of tears.

Stuck in a whirlpool of hopelessness, anger, and desolation, I felt alone. I felt like no one understood what I was going through. Looking back I see now that it was God's grace that drew me back into a prayer I had experienced years before, and that prayer was the one that finally helped me feel connected, understood, and hopeful.

That prayer was the Seven Sorrows Rosary, a contemplative chaplet that focuses on meditating through the seven sorrows Our Lady was asked to face after declaring herself the handmaid of the Lord.

Picture this: A young woman, unimaginably close to God since the day of her conception, was visited by an angel with a plan for her life that she never could have expected or foreseen. She was to bear the Son of God through a great and mysterious miracle. And how did this young woman respond in the face of an event that had never occurred and would never occur again? She said, "Behold, I am the handmaid of the Lord; let it be to me according to your word" (Lk 1:38).

Through her *fiat,* Mary was close to the Lord in a manner surpassing our wildest dreams. She opened herself up to His will in a radical way that would go on to change the history of mankind. She was the first Christian, the model of holiness, the supreme example of abandoning oneself to Divine Providence.

No one throughout history was, is, or will ever be as close to Jesus as she was. So it seems like she should have had a pretty great life, and I think most of us assume she must have had things pretty easy. After all, God would treat the immaculate mother of His Son as we would think she deserved to be treated, right?

Actually, not so much.

The Seven Sorrows Rosary helps us to start to comprehend exactly what happened to the Blessed Virgin Mary after she offered herself unreservedly to God and His will, and this deeply affected me as I went through my darkest of times. Knowing that Mary understood me and my sorrow on such a deep level changed everything for me. As I worked through these seven events in the life of Our Lady, my loneliness was replaced by belonging, my anger was replaced by accompaniment, and my hopelessness was replaced by a longing to understand the good that would come out of the pain.

The seven sorrows of Mary devotion starts with the prophecy of Simeon, where she presented her newborn Son with all the pride of a new parent, only to be told: "Behold, this child is set for the fall and rising of many in Israel, and for a sign that is spoken against (and a sword will pierce through your own soul also), that thoughts out of many hearts may be revealed" (Lk 2:34–35).

She certainly didn't receive the news she expected. Much like my wife and me as the ultrasound technician gave us our son's diagnosis, Mary was devastated to hear the prophecy that her newborn son was going to suffer.

Not long after that, the Holy Family had to flee from their native land into Egypt to avoid the attempted murder of the child Jesus. Then a few years later, Our Lord would wind up lost for three days while Mary and Joseph looked for Him with anxiety and worry. The Mother of God, set apart by God for a unique mission from the moment of her conception, faced struggles and difficulties even though she was willing to submit to God all the way.

Post This! Share something on Facebook that helps point to the importance of Mary in our relationship with Christ without resorting to apologetic arguments.

Fast-forwarding to her Son's adulthood, Mary stood by and watched Jesus as he carried His cross to Calvary, wishing she could do anything to save Him but knowing she couldn't. She stood by the cross as He died, held His lifeless body in her arms as tears streamed down her cheeks, and watched helplessly as the stone was rolled in front of His tomb.

Reflecting on these painful moments in the life of Mary helped me so much in my experience with the death of our son. In each of her sorrows, I saw a reflection of my own journey through pain and heartbreak, and it changed me in a dramatic way.

Just like Mary received Simeon's prophecy, we had received our son's fatal diagnosis. And as Mary watched Jesus on the way of the cross, wishing she could take His place and save His life, so I had wanted God to take me instead of my beautiful baby. And, most intense of all, just as Mary held her lifeless Son, my wife and I held our own.

As I contemplated all of this and how it related to my life in the present day, I came to this question: Why would God allow His Mother to undergo such suffering, pain, and sorrow? There had to be a deeper purpose, a deeper meaning. I had been angry at God for allowing suffering in my life, especially at a time when I was trying hard to grow in holiness and relationship to Him, *but I had nothing on Mary* and all that God asked her to go through! How did it all make sense?

Exploring Mary's pain and sorrow in light of my own *was* the answer. I knew there had to be something to this suffering bit if God would let His own mother go through it. He loved her, after all, and loved me too, and I knew it had to make sense somehow. Connecting myself to her suffering, and allowing her into my heart as I walked through my dark valley, was the first step toward showing me the reasons behind suffering and what we could to do with it.

Share This! Hop onto social media and share about a time in your life when your faith brought on some incredibly beautiful emotions — perhaps tears of joy, laughter at God's sense of humor, or an overwhelming sense of peace. Share it now!

Seeing how Mary handled the pain of losing her Son, the very same pain I was experiencing in my life, opened the door for God's grace to flood into my heart. Looking back on the depths of darkness in which I had been suffocating, it is no hyperbole to say that the Blessed Virgin Mary saved my life.

This story, and the seemingly infinite number of stories like it from those with devotion to Our Lady throughout our Church and our world, allow us to share Mary with others and spark their interest in growing into a deeper relationship with her. More than a giant stack of quotes from the Bible, the Church Fathers, or other apologetic resources, what helps people see Mary's role in our lives and in salvation history is our experiences, our emotions, and our personal journeys.

If we can reflect on our personal lives and share what Mary means to us from our hearts, we can do much more than trying to teach and convince people about Mary from external resources. Personal witness, personal example, emotional journeys are important for moving hearts. Conversion often starts with the heart and the head follows, and when it comes to sharing about the Blessed Virgin Mary, this might be the best place to start.

Apologetics Are Important, but ...

I remember my reversion to the Catholic Faith like it was yesterday. With the arrival of our first son, my wife and I realized the importance of living a more authentic life now that we had a tiny human being watching and evaluating our every move. Around the same time, my job slowed down (*like a lot*), and I had entire afternoons with nothing to do. Somehow, this led me to discover Catholic radio, and like so many before me, I stumbled upon the call-in question-and-answer show *Catholic Answers Live*.

This show absolutely blew me away. Questions I had always wondered about, questions I never even considered before, and challenges that I had in my head about the Faith of my childhood were all answered. And not just answered, but answered clearly, effectively, and convincingly. As I continued to listen day in and day out, I became more and more convinced of the truth of the Faith. While I had never actually left, I had most definitely drifted from it in more than a few ways.

And again, like so many before me, I became a quasi-apologist after a few short months of faithfully listening. Once all of my questions and concerns were addressed, I felt like I needed to take those answers and give them to everyone I met. It's tough to admit now, but I became something of a Catholic triumphalist.

I felt like the arguments I had learned by listening to this radio show were air tight, and if someone didn't understand that I was right, they simply weren't being intellectually honest.

I say it's tough to admit now because it's embarrassing to think about my attitude during this point in my faith journey. As I have continued on and met more people at various points on their own journeys, I have come to realize this is the way conversion and reversion work. First we're drifting, unsure of the truth, questioning everything. Next we come to hear and accept the answers to the questions we've had all along, and we feel great peace in being closer to our faith. Third, we became outspoken evangelists. That's not necessarily a bad thing, but it often leads to an "I'm right and you're wrong no matter what you say" state of existence. It doesn't help many of the people we're trying to evangelize because that triumphalist view of things is extremely off-putting and fails to take into account the wide range of experiences people have.

The final phase of the reversion and conversion process is recognizing that everyone brings different experiences to the table, which means we need to actively listen to them and be willing to meet them where they are. It's at this point where we come to realize that apologetics, while valuable and helpful, typically is not the bread and butter of evangelization success stories.

This is because arguments only go so far. Take for example the Catholic teaching of the perpetual virginity of Mary. Engaging in an apologetic debate, you pull out all the information at your disposal, and your non-Catholic Christian friend does the same.

You have probably experienced this in your own life, especially if you were a budding young apologist without any real theological education background like I was. The arguments stall, and you can't move forward. At the end of the conversation, you both go your separate ways without having been moved an inch, and neither of you has any interest in looking into things further.

This is where our feelings come in. Being able to share our personal experience ... how a truth of the Faith has directly impacted us in our own personal lives ... how these truths have made us feel and changed us on a deep level ... these are the conversations that can help lead our friends to something deeper.

People Can't Argue with Our Experience

After my wife and I had our first son, saying we felt in over our heads would be a serious understatement. Combining sleepless nights and medical complications with the overall feelings of worthlessness that most first-time parents feel right out of the gate was a recipe for disaster. There were times when we would just sit and cry, times when we called for help to anyone willing to answer their phones, and times when one of us would try and fail for hours to get our son back to sleep only to have him fall immediately to sleep for the other spouse leading to inexplicable rage erupting from the depths of our depleted self-efficacy.

And most painful of all, we were lonely.

As mentioned earlier in the book, my mother died before my wife and I were married, and while my father was around to support us as best he could, we felt paralyzed by the mere lack of the village we needed to support us. It became quickly apparent that if we were going to plan on having more children, we were going to have to relocate to be near my wife's family. She was one of seven children, and moving up to the Bay Area would ensure plenty of support if we decided to continue to grow our young family.

It just so happened that this all came at the worst possible time in terms of the housing market. We had recently purchased our home in Southern California as the market continued its slide into what has come to be known as the Great Recession, and moving seemed like a pretty unwise financial decision. But when I received a job offer in the Bay Area, we decided the pros of the supportive extended family far outweighed the cons of losing money, and we packed up and moved north.

Since we were still responsible for paying our mortgage until our home sold, my in-laws were gracious enough to allow us to stay with them for free in the meantime. It was such a blessing to have this opportunity, and I know I shouldn't complain, but the commute from their home to my work (112 miles round trip through Bay Area traffic each day) was like a slow, painful death for me. I would leave for work before anyone woke up and arrive back home just in time to tuck our little one into bed. My life devolved into work and sleep, and my wife's life devolved into being alone with our son who at that point wasn't quite capable of being a companion or doing much of anything for that matter.

Meanwhile, the housing market continued to depress, and we weren't getting any offers on our home down south. As happens with these types of situations, we began to wonder if our decision to move was the absolute wrong one. But at that point, it was too late to click "undo" on our life, and we had to press on. It wasn't easy.

Interestingly, I came across a perpetual Eucharistic adoration chapel within a few miles of my work, and in my hopeless desperation, I decided to drop by during my lunch break and plead with Our Lord for some relief. After walking into the chapel and jotting down my intention in the prayer book, I scanned the bookshelf for something to read as I sat before the true presence of Christ in the Eucharist. I was completely unaware that I was about to find a book that would change everything for me.

I had never heard of Saint Louis de Montfort before that moment, but when I saw his book *True Devotion to Mary*, something inside me decided to pull it out and crack it open. I came back to that chapel during my lunch break every day for the next few days, delving into the spirituality of total consecration to Jesus through

Mary as presented by de Montfort, and I decided to embark on the thirty-three-day journey of my own personal consecration to Mary. Going through the preparation for consecration, I slowly began to feel a sense of peace about our situation. I finally felt able to "Cast all your anxieties on him, for he cares about you" (1 Pt 5:7). My worries lifted off my shoulders, and as if it was meant to be, our home sold shortly after I discovered this path of prayer, and we were able to move into our own place.

When I look back on this time in my life, I connect the Blessed Virgin Mary to my peace, my joy, and the way that everything worked out, and I am so grateful for her presence in these moments. It's undeniable that she played a role. Things just lined up too perfectly for anything else to be true.

Sharing the power of Mary's intercession in my own personal experience is more powerful

Snap This! Do you have a personal experience that shows the power of Mary in your life? Post a video sharing your story to help open others to her help in their own lives!

than listing verses from Scripture, more powerful than printing out a papal encyclical, and more powerful than arguing against another's point of view. Our experience means so much, not only to us, but also to everyone we share it with, and once we show them how we've been touched by Mary in our own lives, the doors are opened for them to learn more. Personal testimonies lower the wall of resistance because we're not trying to change someone's mind, we're just trying to share what we've seen, heard, and felt, and that allows the power of the story to get through to those listening so much more effectively.

The Faith Matters Right Here, Right Now

If we want to bring people closer to Our Lord, Our Lady, and the Faith, we have to make sure we show them that Our Lord, Our Lady, and the Faith are relevant to them right here, right now. That doesn't mean caving to the current popular culture at any given time just to get people in the pews, but it does mean showing that the Faith is not just for grandmas, that the New Testament is not just a book about something that happened two thousand years ago, and that Our Lord and Our Lady care for *everyone, everywhere, at every moment in time.*

One of the greatest saints to exemplify this idea is Saint Oscar Romero. Romero served as the fourth Archbishop of San Salvador, El Salvador, from 1977 until his martyrdom while celebrating Mass in late March of 1980. He understood the need to bring the Gospel message into present-day El Salvador, to show the faithful there that Christ came for them, and that His plan for salvation applied directly to their situation all those years later, all those miles away.

"Christ is present now in our history," Romero once said, and he preached that truth with every homily, every radio broadcast. This reminder that God is with us is so important — in the Holy Land two thousand years ago, in El Salvador in the 1970s and '80s, and in your own life and mine right now, in the present day. The relevance of the Catholic Faith, the relevance of the Blessed Virgin Mary in your life and mine, is precisely what people want to hear about. Which means that we have a duty to share how the Faith has impacted us in our lives, and we can do that with a reach beyond our imagination via our social media accounts!

It's the "So What?" of evangelization: Jesus came to bring us the Good News so that salvation could be offered to all, but so what? Perhaps a more nuanced translation of that would be "What does this mean for me in my life *today*?" We can talk about Jesus going to the Cross on behalf of every one of us; we can talk about how we're all children of the Blessed Virgin Mary and loved deeply by her; we can talk about the importance of availing ourselves of the sacraments, daily prayer, and the list goes on and on; but people will still rightly ask: "What does this mean for me in my life *today*?"

Answering this question is the key to evangelization. Sharing our experiences, our feelings, our personal journey strikes at the heart of this question. Yes, apologetics, verses from Scripture, and writings from Tradition are vital and the backbone of everything we believe. But our experiences show people that the Faith matters right here and right now, and if we can get them to see that, mountains will be moved. Social media is absolutely vital to this movement and this mission because it's precisely the way we share in our present time in history. One powerful tweet, one inspirational post, one meaningful image, and the message of the Church can spread around the world in an instant.

7

Retweeting Her Is Retweeting Him

How Our Lady magnifies Our Lord

After nearly nine years of developing the perfect dad bod through a basic plan of French fries, beer, and Netflix, I decided it was time to try and get an exercise routine going. So, before the sun would peek out over the horizon, I would roll out of bed, lace up my barely used Saucony running shoes, and head out the door. It was arduous at first, my body bouncing along with every step, my legs sore beyond belief after years of inactivity, but slowly my body began to get used to the punishment of running around the neighborhood. Eventually, I got to the point where I was running twelve miles per week (and I call this a success). Even my kids were getting in on the fun of their dad dominating the pavement and knocking out morning runs. They cheered me on and patted me on the back as I walked back in the door, dripping with sweat.

Just as I was really coming into my own, I had to spend a

week on the other side of the country for a work trip. With the incredible momentum I had going, I was sure I'd be able to keep up my new routine. I checked into the hotel and scheduled the whole thing in my head: the days I'd be hitting the treadmill (because it was unbelievably humid that week), and exactly how I'd keep fit until I could return home and get back into the groove. In addition to packing my running shoes, I also packed my Little Office of the Blessed Virgin Mary, a prayer book I had recently begun to use. With my time away from home, I figured I'd have some free periods to delve more deeply into prayer as well.

Share This! Has your devotion to Mary led you closer to Jesus in a tangible way? Share it on Facebook to break the myth that she leads people away from her Son!

Yep, with this trip, I was going to close in on becoming the total package, hitting my prime both physically *and* spiritually. After a few mornings on that Boston treadmill, however, I began to wonder if three runs per week was moving me toward a goal that had any real lasting importance. Sure, I felt much better physically, and it was helping me to work on my gut a bit, but was that the area of my life I needed to work on the most?

It seemed like a random, fleeting feeling. I initially chalked it up to that desperate urge to convince yourself that exercise isn't worth your time that comes around every few months in a workout routine. As I continued to pray the Little Office, however, the feeling proved not to be as fleeting as I initially anticipated. Was Mary trying to tell me something about what I should be doing when I drag myself out of bed in the morning?

When I arrived home from my trip, I handed out the souvenirs to the kids, prayed the Night Prayer from the Little Office, and hit the sack, ready to get back out there on my normal morning running route once the alarm went off. As my phone buzzed me out of bed, however, a thought hit me completely out of the blue before I was able to get my shoes on my feet. I had an inexplicable but intense desire to take a trip to our local perpetual adoration chapel instead of going for my run. I swapped out my (admittedly too short) running shorts for a more appropriate choice and went that very morning. I also went the four mornings after that. Then I had a weekend away with my family, but the two mornings we were gone, I felt a kind of calling. It was weird, if I'm being honest: I had a seemingly inexplicable but seriously overwhelming desire to get myself back into that chapel as soon as possible.

After that, I continued to pray the Little Office and to head straight into the adoration chapel every morning, and I haven't stopped since. While my gut has somewhat returned since the running slowed down, my relationship with Christ has flourished like never before. I went from not really understanding the idea of having a "personal relationship with Jesus" to figuring out exactly what it meant and how it would develop in my own life. As I looked down at the Little Office, kneeling before the True Presence of Our Lord in that chapel, more than one hundred mornings into my daily adoration journey, it hit me: Mary did this.

The random thought to go to adoration one morning instead of running wasn't random at all. My prayers through the Little Office were being heard, my desire to grow closer to the Lord was being answered, and it was all happening by way of a gentle push from "Mom" to adoration. I had been growing in devotion to the Blessed Virgin Mary, praying for her powerful intercession in my life, and she responded as she always does, by placing my focus directly on Jesus. She led me to Him, pulled me by the hand into a deeper relationship with Him through adoration, and there is no possible way to adequately thank her for the impact it has had on my life.

You're Taking the Focus off Jesus

One of the chief complaints about Mary (and all the saints, for that matter) you'll come across on social media is that any attention focused on them is attention that should have been spent focusing on Jesus. "Why would you pray to Mary for help when you could just pray to Jesus directly?" the argument goes, and at face value that seems like a pretty good argument. If we have access to God Himself, why in the world would we send our needs and intentions to another person just so they can bring those needs and intentions to God on our behalf?

Well, thankfully, we don't have to come up with an answer to this question on our own. The Bible has something to say about this, the saints have something to say about this, and God Himself has something to say about this. And, spoiler alert: He agrees with us!

The Bible

In his first letter to Timothy, Saint Paul makes it very clear that we are called to pray for one another: "First of all, then, I urge that supplications, prayers, intercessions, and thanksgivings be made for all men, for kings and all who are in high positions, that we may lead a quiet and peaceable life, godly and respectful in every way. This is good, and it is acceptable in the sight of God our Savior, who desires all men to be saved and to come to knowledge of the truth" (1 Tm 2:1–4).

It's fun to point out to those applying the "one mediator" argument, that the above statement of Saint Paul comes immediately before he talks about Jesus as the "one mediator between God and men." It goes to show that there is no contradiction between Jesus being the sole mediator between God and man and all of us praying on behalf of one another.

Saint James steps up next to help us answer the "Why not go directly to Jesus?" argument. First of all, of course we take our prayers directly to Jesus as Catholics. We pray directly to Jesus every day, and He hears us and imparts His grace and consolation on us in accordance with His will. And yet, asking others to pray for us is a part of His plan as well. Saint James points to one of the reasons why: "The prayer of a righteous man has great power" (Jas 5:16).

Have you ever had a *really big* prayer intention come up in your life? What did you do? Well, if you're like me, you might have done a few things: started praying the Rosary for your intention daily, stopped by the adoration chapel to offer up the prayer in His presence, lit a few candles to symbolize your prayers rising up to God, embarked on a novena specific to your cause, and asked some of the most holy people you know to implore God to help you as well. This is the reason we see so many cute little grandmas constantly praying! They're some of the holiest people around, and they've probably got gangs of grandchildren approaching them and asking them for help.

Snap it! Take a picture of the hymn, "Mary the gate, Christ the Heavenly Way" or better yet, find a recording of the hymn being sung and post it for a social media listening session. (If you're musically inclined, perhaps you could record yourself singing it.)

There's something about a person you regard as holy storming heaven for you. And while we don't believe they have some secret power with Jesus that we don't have, we do recognize that their prayers may come from a place of greater purity, acceptance of God's providence, and holiness that makes them "very powerful." Our grandmothers may be some of the holiest people we know here on earth, but even they can't hold a candle to those who are already in heaven beholding the true presence of God in a manner which we can't even begin to imagine.

This brings us to the final biblical piece of the puzzle, from the Book of Revelation 5:8: " … and the twenty-four elders fell down before the Lamb, each holding a harp, and with golden bowls full of incense, which are the prayers of the saints." This description of heaven shows us very plainly that the saints in heaven are actively praying for us, and if, as Saint James says, the fervent prayer of a righteous person is very powerful, imagine how powerful the prayers of those already in glory with the Lord must be. And so, we reach out to the saints for help in our time of need. And if we're looking for the absolute tops when it comes to holiness among God's creatures, we're reaching out for help to the Queen of All Saints herself, the Blessed Virgin Mary.

All of this is a part of God's plan, not in any way taking away the focus from Jesus but rather showing us just how deeply we are connected to each other as members of His Body. The power of intercessory prayer, be it from a neighbor, a saint, or the Blessed Virgin Mary herself, actually goes to show us just how incredible Jesus and His plan for salvation really are. No one is saved in a vacuum; we are saved in community, and when it comes to imploring Jesus' help through the trials of day-to-day life, it takes that community to bring us closer to Him. And believe it or not, that incredible power of intercessory prayer from those around us may be best seen on social media. Every post on Facebook asking for prayer, every tweet that begs for a Hail Mary for a special intention, all of it leads to scores of people joining in prayer around the world, and when you're the one suffering and in need of that powerful assistance, every reply brings you a sense of peace and consolation.

The Saints

With so many saints having a deep devotion to the Blessed Virgin, you can be assured that they address the argument that looking to Mary takes our focus off Jesus. We'll examine this more in-depth in a later chapter, but for now let's focus on two saints: Maximilian Kolbe and John Paul II.

When Maximilian Kolbe was just twelve years old, he experienced a vision of Our Lady that would radically change the direction of his life. He wrote about that experience: "That night I asked the Mother of God what was to become of me. Then she came to me holding two crowns, one white, the other red. She asked me if I was willing to accept either of these crowns. The white one meant that I should persevere in purity, and the red that I should become a martyr. I said that I would accept them both."

Post This! Have you ever started a devotional practice without realizing at first that you were being pulled in that direction by God? Share it!

It should come as no surprise that he went on to become one of the greatest Marian saints of all time. Kolbe joined the Franciscan order and made his final vows in 1914. Just three years later he would establish the now famous Militia Immaculatae, known in English as the Knights of the Immaculata. The purpose of the group is to bring people back to an understanding of the importance of Mary, her Immaculate Conception, and devotion to her. In 1938, Kolbe explained the group's mission thus: "The purpose of the Knights is contained in these words: to do all you can for the conversion of sinners, heretics, schismatics and so on, above all the Masons, and for the sanctification of all persons under the sponsorship of the Blessed Virgin Mary, the Immaculate Mediatrix."

Most of us know Saint Maximilian Kolbe for his selfless act of bravery when he accepted death at the hands of the Nazis so a man with a wife and children could be spared. But Kolbe also stands as one of the greatest lovers of the Blessed Virgin to ever walk the face of the earth.

On the topic of love Mary, Kolbe was very clear: "Never be afraid of loving the Blessed Virgin too much. You can never love her more than Jesus did." His response is such a beautiful and peaceful one for all of us. Jesus loved His mother perfectly (and continues to do so, in heaven). There is absolutely no way any of us, no matter how deeply we dive into the waters of authentic Marian devotion, can love Mary more than He does. And! No matter how much we honor Mary, talk about her, and share our love of her and the role she plays in salvation history, it can never surpass the honor shown to her by God Himself by selecting her as the immaculate mother of His only Son.

That's it. Nothing can ever top it. We have no need to worry about giving her too much appreciation.

Since most of the great Marian saints will be covered in a later chapter, I'll keep it short here by turning lastly to Pope Saint John Paul II. He developed a love and devotion to the Blessed Virgin Mary at a young age after the death of his mother, and he maintained that close relationship throughout his life, sharing it with the entire world during his pontificate.

John Paul II said *a lot* about Our Lady (we'll consider more of that in chapter 9), but for the sake of brevity and keeping the focus on the specific aim of this chapter, one quote in particular sticks out: "Nothing can be dangerous for us; neither Satan nor the world, nor sin — if there is in us the power of Christ in the Marian way."

Despite what many assume, it isn't all about Mary. When we focus on Mary, we are focusing on Christ in a Marian way, precisely as John Paul II expressed it. In other words, we are focusing on Christ through Mary and with Mary.

The Magnificat

And Mary herself teaches us that her role is all about giving glory to God in her Magnificat in the Gospel of Luke (1:46–55,

NABRE):

> My soul proclaims the greatness of the Lord;
>   my spirit rejoices in God my savior.
> For he has looked upon his handmaid's
>   lowliness;
>   behold, from now on will all ages call me
>   blessed.
> The Mighty One has done great things for me,
>   and holy is his name.
> His mercy is from age to age
>   to those who fear him.
> He has shown might with his arm,
>   dispersed the arrogant of mind and heart.
> He has thrown down the rulers from their
>   thrones
>   but lifted up the lowly.
> The hungry he has filled with good things;
>   the rich he has sent away empty.
> He has helped Israel his servant,
>   remembering his mercy,
> according to his promise to our fathers,
>   to Abraham and to his descendants forever.

You guys, Mary literally says "My soul proclaims the greatness of the Lord," how could it be any clearer? Her Magnificat is such a powerful and moving Scripture passage for us to explore.

"My soul proclaims the greatness of the Lord; my spirit rejoices in God my savior."

Our Lady kicks off her response to her cousin Elizabeth by pointing out that she exists to show forth the greatness of God. She isn't in this for her own glory but for His.

"For he has looked upon his handmaid's lowliness; behold,

from now on will all ages call me blessed."

Mary calls herself God's handmaid, bringing up again her response to the angel Gabriel at the Annunciation that changed the course of salvation history. Then she notes that she will be called blessed because of her lowliness — in other words, her dedication to Him and complete dependence on Him and His plan for her life. She shows us that it isn't the powerful and mighty who will be considered blessed in the kingdom of God, but the lowly and humble. (Also, I like to use this part of the passage to show that everyone should be calling her the *"Blessed* Virgin Mary," not just Catholics. The Bible says so!)

Snap It! Take a photo of the Magnificat (or make your own digital prayer card) and share it on Instagram. It's a powerful prayer that many don't think of when they try and think of their favorite Marian shout-outs — and it's the one prayer we have in Mary's own words.

"The Mighty One has done great things for me, and holy is his name. His mercy is from age to age to those who fear him."

Mary doubles down on her acknowledgment that God has done *everything* that is great for her, in her, and through her. Her accomplishments and her role in salvation history are not of her own making, but only because of God, because of who her Son is. She knows it, she wants all of us to know it, and the Holy Spirit wants all of us to know it. Catholics are often accused of putting Mary on an equal level with God, but from the very beginning, from the very first moment of her public pronouncement of her role in God's plan, Mary makes it clear as can be: God has done great things for her; she has not accomplished any of this by herself.

"He has shown might with his arm, dispersed the arrogant of mind and heart. He has thrown down the rulers from their thrones

but lifted up the lowly. The hungry he has filled with good things; the rich he has sent away empty."

Mary shows us that God has come for the humble, the lowly, the hungry, poor, and marginalized. If ever there was a rallying cry for the Catholic Church's social teaching, this portion of Mary's Magnificat would most certainly be it. Again, Mary is showing us that God is here for those left as outsiders in our society, those deemed disposable and unwanted by the leaders in our world. God comes to us to lift up the lowly and bless those who are thought of as less-than. Mary connects herself with these beloved children of God, with all of us, by showing herself as an example of the lowly who have been raised up.

"He has helped Israel his servant, remembering his mercy, according to his promise to our fathers, to Abraham and to his descendants forever."

Every year during Advent, Catholic social media lights up with debate about the song "Mary, Did You Know?" I think this argument could be put to rest if we just read the Magnificat. Here Mary says plainly that the child conceived in her womb is the very promise God made to Israel. She knew who Jesus was, my friends, so let's stop singing that song.

Mary's humble and yet powerful Magnificat is not only a beautiful prayer, it is also a great biblical proof text, showing that Mary points us to her Son. Devotion to Mary doesn't take our attention away from Jesus. Far from it! This devotion focuses our attention on Mary, who proclaims the greatness of Our Lord and magnifies our focus on God our Savior.

God Wants It to Be This Way

And here's the final point when we set out to prove that devotion to Mary leads us to Jesus: God wants it to be this way.

God is God, of course, and being God, He could have brought Jesus into the world by any means He wanted. If God wanted, He could have had Jesus just pop up on the scene in his early thirties proclaiming the Gospel. There was no specific need for God to come to us in the manner He did, carried in a woman's womb, delivered in what appeared to be a normal human birth, and growing up into his adult years like the rest of us.

And yet, that is the way he chose to do things. That was His plan. *God brought Jesus to all of us through the Blessed Virgin Mary.*

Saint Louis de Montfort put it much better than I ever could: "The Most High God came down to us in a perfect way through the humble Virgin Mary, without losing anything of his divinity or holiness. It is likewise through Mary that we poor creatures must ascend to almighty God in a perfect manner without having anything to fear."

We see again and again in Scripture, and even more profoundly in our daily lives and experiences, that God uses people to bring His grace and salvation into the world. He does it when we come across the story of a saint that inspires us. He does it through the priest who consecrates the bread and wine at Mass. He does it through our neighbors who pray for us when we are in need. And He does it (most especially) through the Blessed Virgin Mary who said yes to bringing our Savior into the world.

When you think about it in that way, it seems only right and just that we would grow in relationship with Him using the same route that He took to offer a relationship and salvation to us: through her.

Mary the Gate, Christ the Heavenly Way

After we got married but before we had kids (a truly magical period in life, filled with all kinds of free time that I didn't appreciate enough), my wife and I started a small weekly prayer group with friends. We rotated who hosted and who picked the prayers, and each week we sat around talking about faith for an hour or so.

It was a blessing to have this time together to grow in our prayer life with friends, and an always interesting weekly experience that I won't forget. Taking turns for picking and running the prayer group was also an underrated blessing, as certain friends with spiritualities different from mine would pick prayers I never would have thought I'd appreciate, and yet in the context I was able to experience their benefit.

One of the prayers that I would often print out when it was my turn to lead the group was actually a mid-twentieth century hymn composed in 1949 by Father Justin Mulcahy, a Passionist priest. This hymn beautifully describes the truth about Mary pointing us to Christ.

I sometimes use this hymn on social media, too. When my mentions on social media are full of the argument that Mary takes my focus away from Jesus, I like to paste these words into my reply. No, they aren't words inspired by the Holy Spirit. No, they aren't official Church teaching on the relationship between Our Lord and His Blessed Mother. No, they probably aren't going to lead to a dramatic conversion where the troll immediately signs up for RCIA and sends me a DM to ask me to be their confirmation sponsor. But this hymn is a powerful, non-threatening way to see what many of us with a strong Marian devotion believe. These words from Father Mulcahy take a poetic approach to our understanding of what Mary does, who she is, and how it is all related to Christ.

Perhaps the fine folks in my mentions keep scrolling after a brief dismissive glance at the hymn, but maybe, *just maybe*, it has planted some seeds, increased some understanding, and moved at least one person to consider the Catholic position on the matter.

Our Experience
Just like sharing our experiences is often more effective for evangelization than sharing apologetics and tactical arguments, our

experiences can also help us determine if certain claims are true or not. As Saint Paul urges us: "Test everything; hold fast what is good" (1 Thes 5:21).

And so we reflect on our own experience: Has deepening our devotion to Mary taken us further away from Christ or brought us closer to Him? As I mentioned in my personal story at the beginning of this chapter, it was precisely my devotion to Mary that brought me into a closer relationship with Jesus through daily trips to our parish's perpetual adoration chapel.

Tweet This! Do you love the song "Mary, Did You Know?" or absolutely loathe it? Either way, tweet your thoughts on the hymn and brace yourself for the replies.

As I look through the whole of my entire life, I see instances of her bringing me closer to Him again and again and again.

And taking it from the personal to the more universal, she is directly responsible for bringing Jesus to every single one of us through her *fiat*. She gave birth to the One who created everything that exists. Our experience all leads us to the fact that Mary points us to Our Lord, and she attributes nothing to herself; she only serves to reflect her Son's greatness and help us grow closer to Him.

8

@ her next time

The importance of praying to Our Lady and
how to deepen your prayer life with her

Sophomore year in high school was a time unlike any other.
My voice was finally starting to stay steady without the high-
pitched cracks (for the most part); I was driving my mom back
and forth to the grocery store as often as she wanted thanks to
my shiny new learner's permit; and I finally had an opportunity
to select some electives in school just because I found them interesting, not because I had to take a certain class to graduate.

Truly, a golden time in life.

One of the classes I signed up for was AP psychology, in part
because it seemed like an interesting subject and in part because I
had heard from those who had just wrapped up their sophomore
year that it was an easy A. I had absolutely no idea that this seemingly random class would set my life off in a direction I still walk
to this very day. *I absolutely loved it.*

The teacher was an eccentric older lady who seemed to be
completely unaware of the high jinks going on in her classroom

full of teens. Most of my classmates were also there for the easy A, but as we read through the textbook and dove into real-life examples of human psychology, cognition, and mental illness, I was completely captivated. It wasn't long after the first day in that poorly ventilated portable trailer in the parking lot of my high school that it hit me: *This is what I want to do with the rest of my life.*

I went into my first year at UC Santa Barbara already sure that I wanted to obtain a degree in psychology. Eventually, I found myself chasing a graduate degree in clinical psych, en route to realizing my dream of becoming a marriage and family therapist. Once I completed grad school, I embarked on the seemingly insurmountable journey of collecting three thousand internship hours just to be able to sit for two licensing exams so I could finally call myself an actual, real-life therapist. The exams were notoriously difficult to pass, but I was sure that it would come as naturally to me as everything else on the journey to that point and didn't give it much of a thought.

Share This! Have you ever found great comfort in praying a rote prayer you've known since childhood? Grab your phone and share the prayer and what it meant for you in that moment!

I stepped into the testing center for my first exam and sat down at the computer filled with a confidence I really had absolutely no right to be filled with. After clicking "Yes, I'm sure" for the third time after answering all the questions, I was snapped out of my prideful, dream-like attitude with a message in bright, bold, red capital letters: "FAILED."

I was shocked. I sat and stared at the screen, absolutely stunned, for what felt like an hour. A picture they made me take at the beginning of the test accompanied the message, an up-close photo of me with a big, dumb, confident smile on my face, now mocking me as I read and reread the word: "FAILED."

The proctor eventually had to come into the testing room and help me get up from my chair. She handed me a piece of paper with that same ridiculous picture of myself on it, along with a message indicating that I would have to wait six months before I could take the test again. "Have a wonderful rest of your weekend!" she added, most likely completely unaware of the tragedy that had just taken place in my life.

I stumbled out of the testing center, slumped my way down the staircase, got into my 2000 Toyota Solara, and broke down in tears. Everything I had worked for, everything I felt I was called to do, it all felt like it had been ripped away. It was as if God was saying, "Come on, take this path," and then all of a sudden he jumped in my way and shouted, "JUST KIDDING! HAHA!"

I felt empty.

As I made the long drive from the testing center back down to the house my wife and I had recently purchased, I couldn't stop crying. And as I was trying to see through the tears while barreling down the freeway, I reached into my pocket and pulled out my rosary. I didn't think about it; it just happened. I cried and I prayed, slowly making my way through the sorrowful mysteries, a total and absolute wreck in search of peace and trying to make sense out of my failure.

The tears slowed as I slid the beads through my fingers, and the intense pain of feeing like all the things I had worked for in life were crashing down around me slowly drifted away. As I pulled into the driveway, the intensity had settled down, and while I was still left wondering what I was going to do next, a sense of peace and purpose replaced the initial intense sorrow and frustration. The rosary, a simple little string of beads that was always tucked away in my pocket, reserved at that point in my life for situations where death seemed imminent, came to my rescue in a moment of need.

Our relationship with Mary is like that: She sits patiently, loving us and waiting for us to come back around and call on her, never bitter when we've been gone too long, but always happy to welcome us back into her arms, prodigal children that we are. But just like our relationships here on earth, things aren't going to progress in our relationship with Mary unless we nurture it, spend time with her, and allow her to know us on a deeper and more intimate level. Our trust in Mary is never going to grow unless we share our hopes and fears with her, ask her to come to aid us in our time of need, and thank her for the beautiful gift of grace passing through her hands from her Son to us.

So pick up those beads, read the words of Mary in Scripture, and get to know her better than ever before. And if you want to inspire those around you to do the same: tweet, post, and snap your journey toward growing in a relationship with Mary and her Son, because you never know who might see your journey while scrolling through their feed and be inspired to delve a little deeper as well!

The Top Five Marian Prayers for Going Deeper
The Rosary

If you polled a thousand people and asked them the one prayer they most associate with being Catholic (aside from the Mass), the Rosary would win, hands down. It's the quintessential Catholic prayer, the beads hanging from the rear-view mirror of every Catholic car on the planet, and the absolute go-to when we're in a time of need.

There are two main traditions for the development of the Rosary as that prayer of all prayers for Catholics: the evolution of the prayers of the Desert Fathers and the apparition of Mary to Saint Dominic in the year 1214.

Prayer beads similar to those of the Rosary appeared in third- and early fourth-century Catholicism, often linked to the laity wanting to go deeper in their faith by imitating the prayers of Christian monasticism. The story goes that the Christian monks would pray all one hundred fifty of the psalms each day, and the laity (who usually were unable to read) would substitute an Our Father for each of the one hundred fifty Psalms, using a cord with one hundred fifty knots in it to help them keep count.

As the spiritual practice evolved over time, it eventually morphed into the Rosary we have today, a contemplative prayer focused on the Gospel and the life of Christ, repeating the Our Father, Hail Mary, and Glory Be to help reach that contemplative state.

Tweet This! What's your favorite mystery of the Rosary and why? Hop on Twitter and let us know!

The Dominican tradition around the development of the Rosary is perhaps more exciting. The story goes that in the year 1214, Saint Dominic had a vision of the Blessed Virgin when he was striving busily in his mission to set the Albigensians straight and finding little success. While praying in the church of Prouille, France, he received this message from Mary herself: "Wonder not that you have obtained so little fruit by your labors, you have spent them on barren soil, not yet watered with the dew of Divine grace. When God willed to renew the face of the earth, He began by sending down on it the fertilizing rain of the Angelic Salutation [the Hail Mary]. Therefore preach my Psalter composed of 150 Angelic Salutations and 15 Our Fathers, and you will obtain an abundant harvest."

Praying as Mary taught him, Saint Dominic immediately began to find great success with bringing the Albigensians back to the truth Faith.

However it may have developed, one thing we can all agree on is that the Rosary is a seriously powerful prayer. I've seen its power in my own life, you've most likely seen it in yours, and saints down through the ages have encouraged the practice of a daily Rosary as a gigantic life hack for growing in the spiritual life ("life hack" being my words, not theirs …).

In fact, Servant of God Sister Lucia, one of the children who literally met the Virgin Mary face-to-face in the little town of Fátima, Portugal, in 1917, would grow up to say, "There is no problem, I tell you, no matter how difficult it is, that we cannot resolve by the prayer of the Holy Rosary."

And if you think that's something, how about the Marian main man himself, Saint Louis de Montfort, who once said:

> If you say the Rosary faithfully until death, I do assure you that, in spite of the gravity of your sins you shall receive a never-fading crown of glory. Even if you are on the brink of damnation, even if you have one foot in hell, even if you have sold your soul to the devil as sorcerers do who practice black magic, and even if you are a heretic as obstinate as a devil, sooner or later you will be converted and will amend your life and will save your soul, if — and mark well what I say — if you say the Holy Rosary devoutly every day until death for the purpose of knowing the truth and obtaining contrition and pardon for your sins.

And how about Pope Leo XIII: "The Rosary is the most excellent form of prayer and the most efficacious means of attaining eternal life. It is the remedy for all our evils, the root of all our blessings. There is no more excellent way of praying."

That's it, folks. There is no more excellent way of praying. If we want to develop a relationship with Mary (and with Jesus through her), the Rosary is a great place to kick things off. That being said, the Rosary isn't everyone's jam, and that's okay. Too often in Catholic corners of the world we can be made to feel as though there is only one path to growing in holiness, to being "the right kind of Catholic." In reality, not all Catholics pray the Rosary.

We're all different; it's part of what makes the Faith and the world so beautiful. And part of being different is practicing different spiritualities. While some may feel called to the Rosary, others may feel called to novenas or *lectio divina* or deep and thoughtful contemplation before the Blessed Sacrament. So if you're wanting to grow in relationship with Mary and not feeling the Rosary, never fear, we're just getting started.

The Memorare

Not to be outdone by the Rosary, the Memorare also has multiple accounts of its creation. For those who may need a refresher, the most common version of the Memorare is:

> Remember, O most gracious Virgin Mary, that never was it known that anyone who fled to your protection, implored your help, or sought your intercession, was left unaided. Inspired by this confidence, I fly unto you, O Virgin of virgins, my Mother. To you do I come, before you I stand, sinful and sorrowful. O Mother of the Word Incarnate, despise not my petitions, but in your mercy, hear and answer me. Amen.

Memorare is the Latin word for "remember," but it seems that history has a hard time remembering this prayer's origin story. Often this wonderful prayer is attributed to Saint Bernard of Clairvaux, but that seems to be a mistake, as the prayer was made popular in the seventeenth century by a French priest named Father Claude

Bernard. Father Claude told everyone that he learned the prayer from his father, which would seem to settle the matter … but not so fast!

History suggests that the Memorare may have actually come from the great Saint Francis de Sales during a time when he felt he was losing his soul to the evil one. After being tormented and even getting to the point where he felt he might be eternally damned, he knelt before a statue of the Virgin Mary in a last-ditch effort to save his soul, and the words that came from his lips were the words of the Memorare. Saint Francis de Sales attributed the salvation of his soul — and a major turning point in his life — to this prayer. He went on to pray it every single day, moving forward in recognition and appreciation of the fact that Mary did not leave him unaided.

Post This! Get on Facebook and paste in the Memorare for all to read and pray. It is, without a doubt, one of the most intense and powerful Marian prayers out there!

Wherever it came from, the Memorare is a powerful prayer. In fact, whenever the going gets really tough and I find myself in a hopeless spot, it's the prayer I pull out of my Catholic toolbox to help get the job done. It recognizes the power of Mary, that all of God's grace flows to us through her. It is a prayer of confidence that Mary will hear our request and help us as our very own mother (since that's who she truly is). It admits that we come to her as sinners in need of God's mercy, and it wraps up by asking that she hear our prayers and bring them before her loving and all-merciful Son to answer in a way that aligns with His will and providence.

It's short, it's powerful, it packs quite a punch; now all you have to do is learn it!

The Magnificat

We covered the Magnificat and broke it down line by line in the previous chapter, but it's worth revisiting briefly again here. (If you want to read it again, turn back to page 101 and then return to here.) Whenever we're at Mass on a Marian feast day and the Magnificat shows up as one of the hymns, you better believe I'm doing all I can to keep myself from standing up on the pews as we sing, *"Aaand holy, hooooly, holy is His name."* There's just something so incredibly special about praying the actual words of Mary, the divinely inspired proclamation of what her *fiat* was about to accomplish, for the descendants of Israel and all of humanity.

And as I mentioned earlier in the book, these words of Mary are powerful, ready to rise up, strike down the rulers, and overturn the many unjust systems of our world. Precisely because of the powerful message, the Magnificat has literally been banned from certain countries at certain points throughout history.

Jason Porterfield shared the history behind this on the website *Enemy Love*:

> During the British rule of India, the Magnificat was prohibited from being sung in church. In the 1980s, Guatemala's government discovered Mary's words about God's preferential love for the poor to be too dangerous and revolutionary. The song had been creating quite the stirring amongst Guatemala's impoverished masses. Mary's words were inspiring the Guatemalan poor to believe that change was indeed possible. Thus their government banned any public recitation of Mary's words. Similarly, after the Mothers of the Plaza de Mayo — whose children all disappeared during the Dirty War — placed

the Magnificat's words on posters throughout the capital plaza, the military junta of Argentina outlawed any public display of Mary's song.

Yeah, Mary is pretty much the best.

The Salve Regina

Speaking of Marian prayers turned into hymns that get me up out of my pew with excitement and joy during Mass on Marian feast days: The Salve Regina may be the preeminent Marian prayer (although I'm realizing I've said that for every single prayer so far …). Here's the traditional Latin text:

> Salve Regina, Mater misercodiae, vita, dulcedo
>   et spes nostrae salve.
> Ad te clamamus exsules filii Hevae.
> Ad te suspiramus gementes et flentes in hac
>   lacrimarum valle.
> Eia, ergo, advocata nostra, illos tuos
>   misericodes oculos ad nos converte.
> Et Iesum benedictum, fructus ventris tui, nobis
>   post hoc exilium ostende.
> O clemens, O pia, O duclis Virgo Maria.
> Ora pro nobis Sancta Dei Genitrix.
> Ut digni efficiamur promissionibus Christi.
> Amen.

And for those playing at home who may not be as proficient in Latin as they pretend to be when they're logged into Catholic social media:

> Hail, holy Queen, Mother of mercy, our life, our
>   sweetness and our hope.

To thee do we cry, poor banished children of
   Eve.
To thee do we send up our sighs, mourning and
   weeping in this valley of tears.
Turn then, most gracious Advocate, thine eyes
   of mercy towards us.
And after this, our exile, show unto us the
   blessed fruit of thy womb, Jesus.
O clement, O loving, O sweet Virgin Mary.
Pray for us O Holy Mother of God,
That we may be made worthy of the promises
   of Christ.
Amen.

What a prayer!

Most likely going back to the eleventh century, the Salve Regina quickly became an important prayer within Catholic liturgy and spirituality in general. Not only did it become the final prayer said after the completion of the Rosary, but it was also incorporated as the final prayer to be said after Compline within the Liturgy of the Hours. Imagine how many people around the world all throughout the day are tossing this one up to the most splendid Queen of Heaven, confident that she will turn her eye of mercy toward all of us as we strive to accept the grace of her Son to guide us to heaven.

Snap It! Take a video of yourself singing the "Salve Regina" (or the "Hail, Holy Queen" in English, if your Latin is kind of rusty) and share it to help inspire a holy singalong online.

If we are to believe the stories of its history, the prayer comes from a Benedictine monk named Blessed Herman the Cripple. Disabled from his youth in various ways, Herman became a monk around the age of twenty, and after losing his sight, he began spending most of his time composing hymns to be used in prayer. The Salve Regina is the one that became his most well-known, and what an incredible legacy Blessed Herman has for himself.

There are few things more efficacious when it comes to humbling ourselves and reaching out to the heavenly host for our intentions than recognizing the Blessed Virgin Mary as queen and thanking Jesus for the incredible graces He bestowed upon her. So get on it!

The Seven Sorrows

My wife and I drove across town to a friend's home for a small prayer group and were surprised when he handed us a little blue pamphlet and something that looked like a rosary, but with too many Our Fathers and too few Hail Marys. I had that weird feeling many of us Catholics have when we're presented with a new prayer we haven't come across before: "Wait ... what's this and why haven't I heard of it?"

That prayer was the Servite Rosary, also known as the Seven Sorrows of Mary or the Seven Dolors. Our friend was a graduate of Servite High School, a very proud Catholic boys high school in Orange County, California, and thus was attached to this form of contemplative prayer. As we walked through the meditations, thumbing the beads through each of the Hail Marys and Our Fathers, it really hit home that this was an incredibly powerful prayer.

The Servite Order was founded in 1233 when a group of merchants in Italy left their wealthy lives behind and moved away from the town to live lives of penance, poverty, and prayer. They donned religious habits similar to the Dominicans, began to live under the rule of Saint Augustine, and devoted themselves to prayer through the Seven Sorrows of Mary.

And if that wasn't enough of a reason to get you ready to order this rosary and start praying, brace yourselves: In 2001, the local bishop of Kibeho, Rwanda, officially recognized a Marian apparition that took place there in 1981 as authentic, and it's connected to the Seven Sorrows Rosary. The Blessed Virgin Mary appeared to three teenagers, declaring herself to be *"Nyina wa Jambo,"* which means "The Mother of the Word." The teens reported that Mary asked for prayer to help prevent a terrible war, and the apparitions included visions of violence, terror, and potentially a foretelling of the Rwandan genocide that was to come. Alphonsine Mumureke, the principle seer of these apparitions, was told to focus on prayer and mortifications. She was teased by the other children of the area, most especially Marie Claire Mukangango. By the grace of God's plan, Marie Claire eventually began to experience

Share This! Do you have a favorite Marian chaplet in addition to the Rosary? Share it online to inspire others to try it out!

the apparitions as well, and it was to her that Mary advised praying the Seven Sorrows Rosary to obtain the favor of repentance.

The reports of the apparitions at Kibeho are inspiring, encouraging, and beautiful all rolled into one, and if Mary asks us to pray, we better get on it!

What If You Aren't Feeling It?

But even with a list of power-packed Marian prayers to help us grow closer to Our Lord and Our Lady, sometimes we just aren't feeling it. What then? It happens a lot, and it's something we're all going to have to face and work our way through from time to time. Even some of the greatest saints among us have gone through periods where they just weren't feeling it, yet they persevered, and that's part of what sets them apart as holy women and men.

First things first: Cut yourself some slack. Yes, you read that right, and yes, this is still a Catholic book. While "Catholic Guilt" has become something of a punchline down through the genera-tions, there's some truth to it. Many of us get down on ourselves when we aren't feeling the Faith in a way that we think we're sup-posed to. If my mind wanders during the Rosary (which, in full disclosure, it does almost every time), I feel guilty that I wasn't doing it right. If I make it to Mass in the midst of suffering in my life and can't bring myself to sing, "Glory to God in the highest" because I'm not feeling that way based on what's happening at the moment, I feel like I'm turning my back on Him. This is why I come back to one of my most frequently given pieces of advice to fellow Catholics (and, as you can see, one that I should really consider taking myself): Let's all cut ourselves some slack.

While I can't judge the innermost regions of your heart, and you can't judge mine (although I'm pretty open with sharing them on social media, if you're interested), I can say based on ex-perience that all of us striving to live an authentic Catholic life in accordance with God's plan are trying our best. Instead of feel-ing guilty because I'm unable to respond at Mass in the midst of heartbreak and pain, I should thank Jesus for giving me the grace to even be at Mass in the first place. Instead of getting down on myself after my mind wanders to the many responsibilities piling up for the day while I pray the Rosary, I should thank God that He has given me the grace to continue working my way through the mysteries despite all the tasks I've got waiting on my checklist for the day.

So, what have I done when I wasn't feeling it to help get me over the hump? One of the biggest solutions was asking people to pray for me. I know, if you're like me that already sounds like an overwhelming solution. If I don't feel up to praying to God my-self, how in the world am I going to be able to tell someone what I'm going through and ask them to pray on my behalf? I'll admit, it isn't easy, but I can also say that texting and social media has made it just a bit easier. I can hop on Twitter and post something as simple as, "If you have a spare moment, would you mind praying an Ave for me?" and the beloved people of Catholic Twitter get right on it. And while I know the power of prayer can often feel muted when we're not having the deep emotional reactions that we hope for, I'm here to tell you *it works*!

When I found myself absolutely unable to pray because I felt like an untrusting fraud given my feelings at the time, the feeling eventually passed after I asked others to pray for me. Telling people I was unable to pray and asking for their help also helped me to be more humble, and it helped me to see the power of the Body of Christ here on earth in a radical way.

When you can't pray, just remember: There are tons of people ready to take up your cause and storm heaven for you. Utilize them!

If you're feeling unable to pray, I also recommend that you take the opportunity to try something different than the memorized prayers for a bit (yes, again, for those who are concerned, this is *still* a Catholic book). When Karen and I were experiencing life after the death of our son, the typical prayers that brought me relief were beginning to feel empty and hollow. At some point, I couldn't even bring myself to pull my rosary out of my pocket. It got to the point where all I could say was, "Jesus, I trust in You." Other than that, it was a lot of conversing with Him and conversing with Mary about what we were going through and what I was feeling.

And you know what? It made me feel a lot better! It felt so freeing to be able to tell it like it is to Jesus and Mary, to really let them have it. Thankfully, they're both more than able to take all the brunt of my frustration, sadness, and anger, and those conversations became a way forward, helping me grow in my faith. If you find yourself not feeling it when you pick up the rosary, tell

Mary! If you find that you're lacking the consolation you feel like you so dearly need when praying that Ave, let her know!

Remember, Mary loves you and cares for you. She's your mother after all, and you know you've got to keep in touch with your mother — or else!

Treat Her Like She's Your Mother

Speaking of Mary being our mother, it's important to take a moment to really drive the point home. I know I've personally fallen into the trap of thinking of Mary as too high, too holy, and too busy to care about me down here on earth with my tiny little sufferings that I blow out of proportion. Too often, I feel like she's not going to want to listen to me when so many of her other children are in such need.

But she's our mother!

No matter what my mother was doing at any given time, no matter how important it was to her, she would always drop it to give me her full attention and to take care of me before thinking of herself. My mom also never missed an opportunity to talk about how proud she was of me, even to the point of embarrassing me, and I think we need to realize that Mary is equally as crazy about us as all of our moms are. And just as our moms have somehow honed the superpower of being able to answer every single request from every single kid, Mary has been given the grace to answer all of her children perfectly.

I will never forget an experience in a local piano shop, where my family was considering buying a piano that we never ended up getting. My mother went on and on telling the piano saleswoman how great of a piano player I was and how quickly I was able to take something I heard on the radio and then play it on my keyboard at home. In reality, I was just an eight-year-old boy who happened to know a couple of songs out of a beginner's book. But my mom loved me like crazy, and she never missed a chance to brag about me to anyone who would listen.

Unfortunately, the saleswoman believed my mother's bragging and excitedly asked me to sit at the piano and show off my skills to the entire store. With my hands shaking from anxiety, knowing full well that I wasn't a quarter of the piano player my mother claimed I was, I sat at this beautiful grand piano and banged out *Ode to Joy* note by note with my right index finger.

"Wow … that's pretty impressive," the saleswoman said with sarcasm so thick even my eight-year-old brain was able to pick it up. My mom, meanwhile, was beaming with pride, completely unaware that I had just embarrassed myself in front of people who actually knew how to play.

I like to think about how Mary is just like my mom, up in heaven leaning over to Jesus and saying, "Watch, he's so holy, you've just got to see this!" And even though Jesus probably watches me with skepticism and wonders what's so special about the tiny little movement toward holiness He just saw, Mary's got a big ol' smile on her face, proud beyond belief about me and every single one of you.

Mary is your mother. Don't forget it!

Ask Jesus to Help You Grow with Mary

Ask Jesus for help in fostering your relationship with His mother. That's what he wants, after all; he showed that plainly to all of us as he hung on the cross: "When Jesus saw his mother, and the disciple whom he loved standing near, he said to his mother, 'Woman, behold, your son!' Then he said to the disciple, 'Behold, your mother!' And from that hour the disciple took her to his own home" (Jn 19:26–27).

I had been reading through Thomas Merton's *The Seven Storey Mountain* every morning in adoration, when I came across an idea that really hit me. It was contained within an exchange between Merton and a friend early in Merton's conversion to Catholicism:

"What do you want to be, anyway?"

"I don't know; I guess what I want to be is a good Catholic."

"What you should say" — he told me — "what you should say is that you want to be a saint."

Merton was taken aback. Could it be that all he needed to do was to decide he wanted to be a saint and ask Our Lord to make it happen, and then boom, it would happen? But in reality, his friend was sharing a profound truth about our relationship with God and the power of Jesus to transform our lives if only we ask for help. In the Gospel, Jesus shares this same truth:

> Ask and it will be given you; seek and you will find; knock, and it will be opened to you. For everyone who asks receives; and he who seeks, finds, and to him who knocks it will be opened. Or what man of you, if his son asks for bread, will give him a stone. Or if he asks for a fish, will give him a serpent? If you then, who are evil, know how to give good gifts to your children, how much more will your Father who is in heaven give good things to those who ask him! (Mt 7:7–11)

Ask Jesus to help you draw closer to Mary. He'll make it happen. And then she'll lead you back to Him, closer than you ever could have imagined.

9

ICYMI (In Case You Missed It)

Sharing the incredible history of Marian apparitions, miracles, and the power of her intercession

Sitting in bed one night as a child, I heard a noise outside my window that sent me into a panic. To be honest, this wasn't a once-in-a-lifetime occurrence. As long as I can remember, I was always scared sleeping alone at night. I would peek out from under the covers, only to be more terrified by the shadows that most certainly looked like something scary inside my doorless closet. (Also, for my parents, *Why would you not have put closet doors on my closet to hide all of those shadows?*) Inevitably, I got up and walked into my parents' room, begging them to let me climb in their bed because this time there really was something scary outside my window. And, inevitably, I was sent back to my own room with the same advice I always got: "There's nothing to be worried about. Pray a Hail Mary and go to sleep."

Praying is a great way to help ease anxiety in most cases, but that night as I went through the prayer, I had a sudden terrifying thought: *What if Mary appeared to me in my bedroom?* As I write this book, I have a hard time understanding why I was scared to have Mary appear in my room (she never did, for those sitting on the edge of their seats), but I can without a doubt remember the fear that was there.

And so, as I prayed the Hail Mary to get some relief from the anxiety I was feeling about the burglar I believed was lurking outside my window (obviously waiting for the perfect moment to come in and commit some terrible crime), I also prayed for Mary not to appear. I'm not sure why I ever thought she might, but I did know that I definitely did not want it to happen.

This is all in spite of the fact that my parents went to lengths to share with me the incredible fruits of Marian apparitions down through the centuries.

Over breakfast the next morning, I told my mom about my concern and about the intensity with which I begged the Blessed Mother not to come. "Oh, Tommy," she responded in that tone only mothers seem to be able to pull off. "If she came, you would be filled with perfect peace, and all your worry would melt away." I kept eating my Grape-Nuts, intellectually convinced my mother was right, but my heart certainly wasn't comforted by her message.

In the childhood years that followed, I continued to ask Mary to take care of me, while at the same time assuring her that she didn't need to make any special visits. I'd take on the burglar myself.

Why Does Mary Appear?

While Mary never stopped by to make an appearance in my bedroom, she most certainly has been stopping by to say hello across the planet down through the centuries. Why? In her 1980s apparition to three children in Rwanda, Mary herself provided the answer to this question. She told seventeen-year-old seer Alphonsine Mumreke, "I love you very much. If I came, it is because you needed it."

We need it. Now, more than ever, we are in need of the message Our Lady brings when she appears here on earth. The consistent themes of her apparitions revolve around turning away from sin, repenting from our evil ways, praying for mercy and for the conversion of the world, and focusing ourselves on her Son, who offers us salvation if only we answer His call to holiness.

Mary appears because we need to be shaken up from our sleepwalking way of life. We hear the commands of Christ in the Gospel every Sunday, we hear the universal call to holiness preached to us through homilies week after week, and yet by lunchtime on Monday, we have drifted back into living on autopilot, failing to make intentional choices to live as Christians in our un-Christian world. We are called to be the light that shines before men, to evangelize through our thoughts, words, and actions, and yet we fail over and over again.

Snap It! Share a picture of your favorite Marian apparition on Instagram and encourage your followers to reply with some of their favs!

I personally have to fight against thinking of the Gospels as a nice little collection of stories from two thousand years ago, a message that has some good ideas but doesn't necessarily apply to our modern world of social media, technology, and comfort. The approved apparitions of Mary throughout the history of the world shake me back into consciousness. They wake me up from my slumber, and they remind me that the Gospel is meant for the here and now in every point throughout history — for you, for me, and for everyone in the world. When Mary touches down on earth and leaves her message (which is really her Son's message) with humble and unknown servants, it reminds me that the supernatural is real, that heaven exists, and that eternity is right around the corner.

Her apparitions help us remember the importance of ordering our lives toward the goal of salvation, urging us to pray for ourselves and for the whole world. They also remind us that we have a loving mother ready to help us at a moment's notice to plead for the mercy that our world so badly needs.

Mary is our star on the sea of life, and her apparitions are helping to guide us home amidst the tumult of that sea to our heavenly homeland.

How Do We Know It's True?

When I was in high school, a local news story about a hometown chocolate maker became the talk of the town. The word on the street was that a piece of chocolate made at the location came out radically different than all the rest: It looked like the Blessed Virgin Mary! The chocolate was immediately taken off the line and placed in a location of prominence within the shop. Droves of people came to the shop to admire, pray, and be in the presence of something potentially from out of this world.

I wanted to go and be a part of the hysteria and excitement around visiting this mysterious piece of chocolate. But as I tried to reconcile my school schedule with the hours the chocolate shop was open, I started to wonder why I wanted to go at all. Did I want to go because I thought it would give me a special connection to Our Lady? Not really. I wanted to go because I thought it'd be cool to get involved in the excitement, because I thought it'd be cool to be able to look back on the story and say *I was there!* It had far less to do with faith and far more to do with FOMO (the fear of missing out). After all, how could anyone know if the chocolate was truly candy sent from heaven or just a misshapen mistake? Even I knew it was more likely the latter. A skeptic at heart, I don't tend to believe the stories of toast looking like Mary, crackers shaped like crucifixes, or even statues found to be weeping blood, tears, or olive oil. I'm usually a "probably not" guy when it comes to this kind of stuff, so I didn't really believe the chocolate was a sign from Mary.

Despite my natural skepticism, I have found great fruits of faith, love, and hope in the various approved apparitions of Mary from around the world. Why?

Why would I believe Mary is trying to communicate with her children in one circumstance, say on Tepeyac Hill in the 1500s, but then not believe the same to be true in my hometown chocolate shop in the late 1990s? The answer lies in the way the Church herself approaches claims of supernatural miracles, visions, and messages. The Church goes out of her way to be skeptical when people claim to receive private revelation, and she always takes a "wait-and-see" approach. Typically, after some time, the local bishop will investigate the claims and put out a tentative statement on its authenticity. But official declarations from the Vatican usually don't come until long after the apparitions have ended so the message can be matched up against the revelation handed to us through Scripture and Tradition, and the fruits of the apparition can be examined.

Since the Church is in the business of the eternal, there is no rush. When it comes to apparitions, the Church wants to be precise and accurate so as to ensure that she is leading the faithful in the right direction. While we may want answers immediately, the Church knows quick decisions aren't always prudent ones. When one examines the fruits of the approved apparitions, it becomes abundantly clear that something incredible has happened in each of these situations, and those fruits are still being experienced generations later.

Even when the Church does approve private revelation, Catholics in good faith are not required to believe it. This comes as a surprise to many, but there is no requirement for Catholics to believe Mary came to visit the children in Fátima, for instance. *She most definitely did,* but we aren't required to believe it.

This is because apparitions are considered private revelation, and private revelation (no matter how important, how incredible, or how helpful) is not binding on all the faithful. Not having to believe it, however, doesn't mean one shouldn't believe it. The Marian apparitions that have occurred down through the ages all contain important messages for each and every one of us. They contain reminders to repent and believe in the Gospel, to give our entire selves to Christ and His Church, and to pray for souls.

Do we have to believe it? No. Will believing and listening to the messages help us in our faith journey? Most certainly, yes.

The Big Three

While there are many approved Marian apparitions to guide and inspire the faithful, three take the cake as the *most* helpful, the *most* inspiring, and the *most* important. These are Our Lady of Guadalupe, Our Lady of Lourdes, and Our Lady of Fátima.

Guadalupe

The year: 1531. A fifty-seven-year-old native of Cuautitlán was on his way to Mass one morning when he was visited by a young woman at Tepeyac Hill who spoke to him in his native Nahuatl language. She identified herself to the man, Juan Diego, as the "mother of the very true deity" and asked for a church to be built at the site of their meeting. Juan Diego went to Bishop Zumárraga to inform him of the meeting and request, but he was not believed.

The young woman was persistent and made the same request of Juan Diego again during a second visit. This time, the bishop instructed Juan Diego to ask the young woman for a sign. Juan Diego did as instructed, and the young woman told him to come back the following day to receive his sign.

On that day, however, Juan Diego's uncle became sick and needed Juan Diego to look after him. The following morning, he set out to find a priest to give his uncle the Last Rites before his passing. He tried to avoid Tepeyac Hill, but the young woman found him. She assured him that there was no need to worry, saying, "*¿No estoy yo aquí que soy tu madre?*" ("Am I not here, the one who is your mother?") She let him know that there was no need for him to get a priest at this time; his uncle would be healed. Then, although it was winter and no flowers should be in bloom, she instructed Juan Diego to gather roses from the top of Tepeyac Hill. He did so, and when he came back down, she carefully arranged them in his tilma and told him to present the flowers to the bishop.

Tweet This! What's your favorite cool fact about the tilma? Tweet it so we can check it out!

The rest, of course, is well-known. When Juan Diego opened up his tilma, the roses spilled out and there for everyone to see was the image of the young woman, the Blessed Virgin Mary, Our Lady of Guadalupe, miraculously imprinted. The bishop and everyone in attendance were absolutely stunned.

The tilma of Juan Diego and the image of Our Lady that was presented to Bishop Zumárraga and everyone else in attendance at that moment in 1531 continues to persist, available for the entire world to see at the Basílica de Nuestra Señora de Guadalupe in Mexico City. It is an incredible testament to Mary's power, and a reminder that heaven is real and that the Mother of God cares about us and loves us even down to this present time.

Lourdes

In 1858, a young girl had a vision of Our Lady in the vicinity of Lourdes, France. The fourteen-year-old Bernadette Soubirous, widely noted to have little experience in terms of education, claimed that she was visited by a woman in white, with a rosary and blue belt fastened around her waist, and two golden roses at her feet.

Bernadette was out collecting firewood with her sister, and the two waded into some water in a nearby grotto. Bernadette recorded what happened next:

> I came back towards the grotto and started taking off my stockings. I had hardly taken off the first stocking when I heard a sound like a gust of wind. Then I turned my head towards the meadow. I saw the trees quite still: I went on taking off my stockings. I heard the same sound again. As I raised my head to look at the grotto, I saw a lady dressed in white, wearing a white dress, a blue girdle and a yellow rose on each foot, the same color as the chain of her rosary; the beads of the rosary were white. ... From the niche, or rather the dark alcove behind it, came a dazzling light.

Bernadette's family and others from the area were skeptical and attempted to keep her from returning to the site of the apparition while interrogating her in an effort to make her admit she had made it all up. Eventually, Bernadette reported that the woman instructed her to dig in the mud and drink from the water that would come up. She did as she was told, much to the dismay of onlookers who found her behavior absolutely odd and off-putting. To everyone's surprise, a spring of clean water bubbled up and became a source of incredible miracles and healings.

Bernadette reported that when asked to identify herself, the woman appearing to her simply responded, "Je suis la conception immaculée" ("I am the Immaculate Conception"), indicating that she was indeed the Blessed Virgin Mary.

Since that time, Lourdes continues to be a place of great miracles. Every year, countless pilgrims visit the Grotto and bathe in the miraculous water there. Approximately seven thousand people have sought to have their healing confirmed as a miracle; of these, sixty-nine have been declared a scientifically inexplicable miracle by the Catholic Church.

Fátima

One of the most well-known apparitions took place in the village of Fátima, Portugal, in 1917. Three young shepherd children, Lucia dos Santos and her cousins Francisco and Jacinta Marto, claimed that they were initially visited by an angel in the summer of 1916. This "angel of peace" encouraged the children to join in prayers he taught them (including the Fátima prayer that you most likely say after each Glory Be during your Rosary), to make sacrifices for sins, and to spend time in Eucharistic adoration.

Post This! Have you ever been blessed to receive holy water from Lourdes? Have you perhaps been to Lourdes (or Guadalupe or Fatima)? Share your experience on Facebook!

As if that wasn't exciting and profound enough, in the spring of 1917 the angel returned, and then a woman appeared to them, "brighter than the sun, shedding rays of light clearer and stronger than a crystal goblet filled with the most sparkling water and pierced by the burning rays of the sun." The woman asked the children to pray the Rosary every day for the intention of peace. In June, she came back and let the children know that Francisco and Jacinta would soon be taken to heaven, but that Lucia would live longer in order to spread her message.

Can you imagine the intensity of that message, and everything still to come?

The woman continued to underscore the importance of praying the Rosary and even revealed a vision of hell to the children while entrusting secrets to them. Officials in the area were incensed as more and more people began to flock there in response to the visions. The officials had the children placed in jail and interrogated them. They hoped to convince them to give up the secrets and to admit that this was all a lie. The children persisted. The next apparition informed the children that in October there would be a miracle that would help to convince the world that what was happening was true. On the predicted day, October 13, 1917, thousands of people (estimates range from thirty thousand to one hundred thousand) showed up in anticipation of what would happen.

And then it happened.

According to accounts, after a period of rain, the dark clouds broke and the sun appeared as an opaque, spinning disc in the sky. It was said to be significantly duller than normal, and to cast multicolored lights across the landscape, the people, and the surrounding clouds. The sun then reportedly careened toward the earth before zig-zagging back to its normal position.

Devotion to Mary as Our Lady of Fátima quickly spread throughout the world and has been extremely popular among Catholics, both for the message she left and because of the interest piqued by the secrets Mary left with the children. No matter where one stands on the issues related to Fátima, one thing is abundantly clear: The apparitions of Mary to the three children in Portugal left a huge imprint on our Church and our world as a whole. There has been a greater devotion to the Rosary and a greater interest in making sacrifice for sins, all thanks to those three little shepherd kids sharing their experience with the one and only Blessed Virgin Mary.

Lesser-Known Apparitions

While these "Big Three" are the ones that spring to mind immediately when most of us think of Mary's apparitions, there are a handful of other, lesser-known events, and they are just as beautiful and inspiring.

La Salette

Just a bit before her visit to Bernadette in Lourdes, Our Lady appeared to two children up the road in La Salette-Fallavaux, France, in 1846. Maximin Giraud and Melanie Calvat were returning from taking care of their family's cows and saw a woman sitting, holding her head in her hands. The woman wore a crucifix around her neck, and as the children approached she spoke to them in French and their own native language of Occitan. The children claimed she gave each of them a secret, and then walked up the hill and vanished.

The message Our Lady wanted to be made public was for everyone to know the importance of respecting the seventh day of the week (keeping Sundays holy) and respecting the name of God. She noted that if these two commandments weren't heeded more carefully, there would be consequences, particularly by way of a potato famine, which indeed took place the next winter in France and Ireland.

Melanie would go on to become a nun, while Maximin led a difficult life that ended in 1875. Saint John Paul II spoke about the apparition on its 150th anniversary, stating, "La Salette is a message of hope, for our hope is nourished by the intercession of her who is the Mother of mankind."

The secrets were never made public, and Maximin and Melanie didn't even share their secrets with each other. The secrets were sent to Pope Pius IX, but they were not shared by him or any other pope since, leading many to form conspiracy theories (as many have also done with the secrets of Fátima).

No matter the secrets, and no matter when or if they will be revealed, the message from La Salette to keep Sundays holy and respect the name of God is one that we should still be pushing for in the present time.

Knock

My fifth-generation Irish heart couldn't let this chapter go by without mentioning Our Lady of Knock! One rainy August night in 1879, Mary Beirne was accompanying the housekeeper of the parish priest back home when she noticed three life-sized figures standing beside the church building. She went to get her parents, and when they all returned, there in the pouring rain, they witnessed Our Lady, Saint Joseph, and Saint John standing beside an altar with a cross, a lamb, and adoring angels all around it.

Over the course of about two hours, the group swelled to twenty-five, all kneeling and taking in the incredible scene. A farmer who was not at the apparition site later reported seeing a golden globe of light in the sky over where the apparition was happening. Of those who were at the site during the apparition, the reports were that the ground beneath the figures stayed completely dry despite the driving rain.

Various healings and miracles have been associated with the site of Our Lady of Knock, and to the present day it continues to be an important spot and source of Marian devotion for the Irish people.

Akita

In 1973, Sister Agnes Katsuko Sasagawa reported that she began to experience apparitions of the Blessed Virgin Mary in the Yuzawadai, Akita Prefecture in Japan. The messages Mary brought were similar to those that have been received through other Marian apparitions around the world. Sasagawa had experienced multiple health problems throughout her life, but reportedly was healed after drinking the water from Lourdes. She eventually went completely deaf, however, and was brought to be cared for by the nuns who lived near Akita.

On July 6, 1973, a statue of Mary became illuminated and instructed Sister Agnes to pray for the healing of her deafness, which would happen later. Mary reportedly told Sister Agnes, "Pray very much the prayers of the Rosary. I alone am able still to save you from the calamities which approach." Later she said, "Many men in this world afflict the Lord. I desire souls to console Him to soften the anger of the Heavenly Father. I wish, with my Son, for souls who will repair by their suffering and their poverty for the sinners and ingrates."

After a third message was received that October, a number of nuns present witnessed the statue of Mary moving. Throughout this time, Sister Agnes received the stigmata, and then in December something unique among Marian apparitions happened. The statue in question began to weep, and the experience was broadcast live on TV by Tokyo Channel 12 throughout the entire country.

The statue became associated with numerous cures and miracles after this. While this apparition is not widely known, it is most definitely a special example of Mary touching down on earth to make a difference in our lives.

Our Lady of Kibeho

Our Lady popped up again in the 1980s in Rwanda, and while still relatively unknown, her message to three children in the area is one everyone needs to hear. On November 28, 1981, Mary first appeared to a young schoolgirl named Alphonsine Mumureke and referred to herself as "Nyina wa Jambo," which means "Mother of the Word." Alphonsine and the two other seers, Nathalie Mukamazimpaka and Marie Claire Mukangango (who initially bullied Alphonsine over the alleged apparitions), continued to experience visitations from Mary up until September 15, 1982.

The message of Mary was similar to other apparitions: She

told the girls to pray and make sacrifices in reparation for sins ... or else. The teenagers reported that Mary told them everyone had to pray to prevent war and destruction from taking place, and many link the visions they experienced to a foretelling of the Rwandan genocide in 1994.

As mentioned earlier, Marie Claire Mukangango was also told about the power of the Seven Sorrows Rosary, and she was encouraged to tell the world to pray it every day.

Here in the United States

Perhaps you wonder why we don't hear about Mary appearing to anyone here in the United States. Our Lady of Guadalupe is obviously deeply important to those of us in the Americas, but while our country is young, wouldn't it be comforting to know that Our Lady had come down to us here and was keeping a watchful eye over us?

Allow me to introduce Adele Brise.

Belgian native Adele Brise immigrated with her family to Wisconsin at the age of twenty-four. Four years after moving to the States, she experienced something that would change her life forever. She reported that she saw a woman standing between two trees, surrounded by a blinding light, with dazzling clothes. She did exactly what I would do in the situation: Out of fear, she prayed for the woman to leave her. After the woman disappeared, Adele ran to her parents and told them what happened. They responded that it might have been a poor soul from purgatory in need of prayers.

The woman reappeared to Adele when she was on the way to

Share This! Do you have a favorite "lesser known" Marian apparition? Hop on social media and tell us which one it is and why it's special to you!

Mass with a sister and a friend. While neither of her companions saw the woman in question, Adele took the information to her parish priest, who advised Adele to ask the woman (if she was to appear again), "In the name of God, who are you and what do you wish of me?" Returning home that same day, Adele got the opportunity to ask the woman that very question. The woman responded: "I am the Queen of Heaven, who prays for the conversion of sinners, and I wish you to do the same." She gave Adele the mission she was to follow for the remainder of her life, to "gather the children in this wild country and teach them what they should know for salvation."

While Adele never took public vows as a nun, she dedicated her life alongside a few other women, going by foot around the local area to teach as many people as she could about the Good News of the Gospel and the message of conversion for the sake of salvation.

Twelve years after the apparition, Adele and a few others were present for what has come to be seen as a miracle through the intercession of Our Lady of Good Help (the title given to this apparition of the Blessed Virgin). A raging fire ripped through the local town, heavily forested by the budding lumber industry. It was an unstoppable inferno that killed two thousand people. As the fire approached the chapel built by Adele's father in Mary's honor, most of those hiding inside the chapel expressed a strong desire to evacuate to save their lives. Adele, confident that they were under the protection of Our Lady, calmed the crowd, encouraged them to stay, and prayed for Mary's help. While the surrounding lands, buildings, and everything around them was destroyed, the chapel remained completely untouched by the flames, and everyone inside the chapel was miraculously safe.

What Do We Do with Medjugorje?

While this is not an approved apparition, Medjugorje is popular and well known, so it is worth mentioning here. Reportedly, the Blessed Virgin Mary appeared in Bosnia and Herzegovina back in 1981, and she is allegedly still appearing today. Many people, probably including people you know personally, feel very positive about the claims of apparitions in Medjugorje. An untold number of great awakenings to the Faith have been reported for those who go on pilgrimage there, and there are many positive stories related to the site, the seers, and the area.

That being said, Medjugorje has not been approved by the Church. Officially, it is still being studied and examined, and while news of a recent Vatican commission to study the initial apparition claims have had people paying attention for the final verdict, if history is any indicator, that verdict may still be a long way off.

While the debate about the authenticity of the Medjugorje apparition lines Catholics up on both sides, the important thing is to remember that our Church is one of generations and centuries. The Church has her reasons for taking time and ensuring that the pronouncements she makes are correct and something the faithful can continue to put their faith in. It's always important to trust in God, love His Blessed Mother, and accept the authority of the Church in such matters.

What Do all the Marian Apparitions Have in Common?

If I had to sum up the message of the entire body of Marian apparitions in one popular internet meme, it would have to be this: *Repent and submit.* But as a way of inviting those on the outside looking in, I think it's vital for us to share our experiences with these Marian apparitions, to help put a personal touch on these historical events and how they're still impacting us today. Tweeting about the miracles from Lourdes, posting to Facebook the video that shows all the incredible and verified qualities of the tilma, going on Instagram Live to share a Rosary with the Fátima prayer handed down to the children from the angel — all of this can open the door to the curious and those who may have always kept these apparitions at a distance.

And when you're sharing, remember that Mary never brings new information or new revelation to the world when she appears. Rather, she seeks to remind us of the urgency with which we should be growing in holiness, praying in reparation for our sins and those of the whole world, and turning our whole hearts to her Son, Jesus Christ.

She's telling us the time is now. She's calling us to pray more, noting that straying from God's plans will lead us to destruction. She's asking us to abandon ourselves to God's providence, to be willing to trust Him, follow Him, and live for Him. Every appearance of Mary, from Akita to Fátima, from Tepeyac to Knock, from Lourdes to Champion, is about Jesus. It's about our mother stopping by to remind us of the reason for our lives, the reason for the hope within us, the reason we persevere and keep putting one foot in front of the other.

Mary most certainly stops by from time to time to pay us a visit here on earth, and she's leaving us with a message focused on turning toward her Son with reckless abandon, because that's what it's all about.

10

Squad Goals

A look at the saints who had a devotion to
Our Lady and what we can learn from them

Less than one week away from my confirmation, I was excited, but also filled with anxiety because I hadn't selected my confirmation saint yet. I pored over the homemade staple-bound book my confirmation teacher handed out and tried my best to rank my potential options while feeling about as overwhelmed as a teenager can at that point in their young life.

Should I pick Saint Christopher? Our book called him the patron saint of rollerblading, and I was obsessed with rollerblading. (It was the '90s, give me a break.) Should I pick Saint Francis of Assisi because my mom's middle name was Frances, and it would be a sweet tribute to her instilling the Faith so deeply in me? Should I just give in and settle on Saint Thomas, since he's literally my patron by name?

When it was all said and done, I selected Saint John the Baptist, mostly because even in my teenage years, his profound humility struck me: "the thong of whose sandal I am not worthy to untie" (Jn 1:27). While I often look back and wish I had picked a more obviously Marian saint, I have slowly started to realize that Jesus' cousin may actually be one of the most Marian saints I could have considered. After all, the first thing we read about him in Scripture is: "And when Elizabeth heard the greeting of Mary, the child leaped in her womb" (Lk 1:41).

You don't get much more cred as a Marian saint than leaping at the sound of her voice while you're still gestating in your mother's womb. That being said, there are plenty of Marian saints waiting to walk with you and help you on your journey toward developing and maintaining a relationship with Mary, and here are just a few for you to introduce yourself to. And as you come to know these saints more closely, as they begin to impact your journey into a deeper relationship with Mary and thus with her Son, be sure to pull out your phone to share how they've helped you. Tweet out about the saint, live stream prayers that your followers can join in on, and spread icons of the saints on Instagram for all to see!

Louis de Montfort

When it comes to Marian saints, few have as much of a right to the title as the one and only Saint Louis de Montfort. Here on earth from 1673 to 1716, de Montfort is best known for developing the Total Consecration to Jesus through Mary, a devotion still practiced by a huge number of Catholics around the world today. He is known as one of the earliest writers in the field that came to be known as Mariology, busting out a ton of books on the subject, most notably *Secret of the Rosary* and *True Devotion to Mary*.

His spirituality can be summed up in a few points:

- "God alone"
- The Incarnation as central to the Faith
- Deep love of the Virgin Mary
- Loyalty to the cross

- A strong zeal to evangelize

Of his devotion to Mary, de Montfort said, "Now, since Mary is of all creatures the one most conformed to Jesus Christ, it follows that among all devotions that which most consecrates and conforms a soul to our Lord is devotion to Mary, his Holy Mother, and that the more a soul is consecrated to her the more will it be consecrated to Jesus Christ."

As I mentioned earlier, I ran into Saint Louis de Montfort and the Total Consecration to Jesus through Mary seemingly randomly in a Eucharistic adoration chapel one day. As I walked through the thirty-three-day preparation and have lived deeply the consecration over the last few years, I have come to realize it absolutely was not a random event. God's grace is always waiting for us, and meeting de Montfort was one of those moments when God intervened in my life in a way that only He knew would shake me up and get me back on the right path, most especially by preparing me for the trials and tribulations that were waiting ahead.

Post This! Do you have a favorite Marian saint not mentioned here? Create an Instagram post (complete with a picture) and tell us all about them and how their Marian devotion inspires you.

Because of that, de Montfort has become one of the most influential saints in my life, and I hope you delve into his life and spirituality yourself to find what he has waiting for you. In the meantime, here's a prayer you might consider praying and even sharing on social media (though it's too long for a tweet):

Saint Louis de Montfort's Prayer to Mary
Hail Mary, beloved Daughter of the Eternal Father! Hail Mary, admirable Mother of the Son!

Hail Mary, faithful spouse of the Holy Ghost! Hail Mary, my dear Mother, my loving Mistress, my powerful sovereign! Hail my joy, my glory, my heart and my soul! Thou art all mine by mercy, and I am all thine by justice. But I am not yet sufficiently thine. I now give myself wholly to thee without keeping anything back for myself or others. If thou still seest in me anything which does not belong to thee, I beseech thee to take it and to make thyself the absolute Mistress of all that is mine. Destroy in me all that may be displeasing to God, root it up and bring it to nought; place and cultivate in me everything that is pleasing to thee.

May the light of thy faith dispel the darkness of my mind; may thy profound humility take the place of my pride; may thy sublime contemplation check the distractions of my wandering imagination; may thy continuous sight of God fill my memory with His presence; may the burning love of thy heart inflame the lukewarmness of mine; may thy virtues take the place of my sins; may thy merits be my only adornment in the sight of God and make up for all that is wanting in me. Finally, dearly beloved Mother, grant, if it be possible, that I may have no other spirit but thine to know Jesus and His divine will; that I may have no other soul but thine to praise and glorify the Lord; that I may have no other heart but thine to love God with a love as pure and ardent as thine. I do not ask thee for visions, revelations, sensible devotion or spiritual pleasures. It is thy privilege to see God clearly; it is thy privilege to enjoy heavenly bliss; it is thy privilege to triumph gloriously in Heaven at the right hand of thy Son and to hold absolute sway over angels, men and demons; it is thy privilege to dispose of all the gifts of God, just as thou willest.

Such is, O heavenly Mary, the "best part," which the Lord has given thee and which shall never be taken away from thee — and this thought fills my heart with joy. As for my part here below, I wish for no other than that which was thine: to believe sincerely without spiritual pleasures; to suffer joyfully without human consolation; to die continually to myself without respite; and to work zealously and unselfishly for thee until death as the humblest of thy servants. The only grace I beg thee to obtain for me is that every day and every moment of my life I may say: Amen, So be it — to all that thou didst do while on earth; Amen, so be it — to all that thou art now doing in Heaven; Amen, so be it — to all that thou art doing in my soul, so that thou alone mayest fully glorify Jesus in me for time and eternity.

Amen.

Dominic

If we're talking Marian saints, we absolutely have to cover Saint Dominic, founder of the Order of Preachers (better known as the Dominicans), and a saint with a deep and profound devotion to Our Lady.

Dominic lived between 1170 and 1221, and he showed signs of holiness from a young age. While a famine swept across his native Spain in 1191, Dominic became well-known for giving away all of his money, as well as selling everything he had to help feed the hungry. Fast-forwarding to 1215, Dominic and six followers established the Order of Preachers under Pope Honorius III in 1217.

As for Dominic's Marian devotion, Pope Pius IX once said, "The Rosary of Mary is the principle and foundation on which the very Order of Saint Dominic rests for making perfect the life of its members and obtaining the salvation of others." The story goes that the Blessed Virgin Mary appeared to Saint Dominic in the year 1214, and while it may be disputed by some, what absolutely cannot be disputed is the fact that Saint Dominic and his followers had a central role in spreading devotion to what can now be called *the* Catholic prayer, outside of the Mass — the string of beads most of you probably have hanging from your car's rearview mirror.

Share This! Who was your confirmation saint and what led you to select them? Share the story on Facebook!

Take this as a sign that you need to grab them from there and start praying! And here's a prayer to Saint Dominic that you can pray yourself and share with your social media followers, especially on or near his feast day (August 8):

A Prayer to Saint Dominic

I. O glorious Saint Dominic, thou who wast a model of mortification and purity, by punishing thy innocent body with scourges, with fastings, and with watchings, and by keeping inviolate the lily of thy virginity, obtain for us the grace to practice penance with a generous heart and to keep unspotted the purity of our

bodies and our hearts.
Our Father, Hail Mary, Glory Be

II. O great Saint, who, inflamed with divine
love, didst find thy delight in prayer and
intimate union with God; obtain for us to be
faithful in our daily prayers, to love Our Lord
ardently, and to observe His commandments
with ever-increasing fidelity.
Our Father, Hail Mary, Glory Be

III. O glorious Saint Dominic, who, being
filled with zeal for the salvation of souls, didst
preach the Gospel in season and out of season
and didst establish the Order of Friars Preachers to labor for the conversion of heretics and
poor sinners, pray thou to God for us, that He
may grant us to love all our brethren sincerely
and to cooperate always, by our prayers and
good works, in their sanctification and eternal
salvation.
Our Father, Hail Mary, Glory Be

V. Pray for us, Saint Dominic,
R. That we may be made worthy of the promises of Christ.
Let us pray.
Grant, we beseech Thee, Almighty God, that
we who are weighed down by the burden of our
sins may be raised up by the patronage of blessed Dominic Thy Confessor. Through Christ
our Lord.
Amen.

Hildegard

Saint Hildegard of Bingen is easily one of the most underrated saints in our beloved Church. Here on earth from 1098 to 1179, Saint Hildegard was known as a polymath, which is basically like being an absolutely mind-blowing Renaissance woman. She was an abbess, writer, composer, philosopher, mystic, visionary, and is considered to be the founder of scientific natural history in Germany.

She also wrote liturgical drama, theological texts, botanical books, medicinal tomes, liturgical hymns, and vast amounts of poetry. And to top it all off, she was a saint of deep Marian devotion.

Hildegard placed great emphasis on the Incarnation and utilized language in her writing describing Mary as a tabernacle: "This means that the Son of God with the brightness of his divinity took on the flesh from the Virgin who existed like a tabernacle for another life for the salvation of the human race. For God is called the burning sun that illuminated everything at the time of creation; from the heat of the sun, the flesh of the Virgin, like a tabernacle, grew warm so that a man with a brighter faith and with a more burning charity came from it in the same way that God joined Eve to Adam before the fall."

And her beautiful words about Mary continue in her work *Scivias*: "And on her breast shines a red glow like the dawn; for the virginity of the Most Blessed Virgin when she brought forth the Son of God glows with the most ardent devotion in the hearts of the faithful. And you hear a sound of all kinds of music singing about her: 'Like the dawn, greatly sparkling;' for, as you are now given to understand, all believers should join with their whole wills in celebrating the virginity of that spotless Virgin in the Church."

Hildegard's beautiful writing still stands out to this very day, and her words about Mary inspire imagery that can have all of us meditating for quite some time.

> **Prayer to Saint Hildegard**
> O God, by whose grace your servant Hildegard,
> kindled with the Fire of your love, became a
> burning and shining light in your Church:
> Grant that we also may be aflame with the spir-
> it of love and discipline, and walk before you as
> children of light; through Jesus Christ our Lord,
> who lives and reigns with you, in the unity of
> the Holy Spirit, one God, now and for ever.
> Amen.

Anthony

I would be in a whole heap of trouble with my mother-in-law if I left her favorite saint off of this list. Saint Anthony of Padua lived from 1195 to 1231 and is best-known as the patron saint of lost items. He was an incredible preacher with an amazingly deep faith that led to countless conversions.

As a story goes, Anthony attempted to preach to some people only to find them unwilling to listen. In a sign of profound trust in God, he turned to the sea and began to preach the Gospel to the fish. Much to the surprise of those who wouldn't at first lend him their ears, the fish of the sea began to come to the surface and listen to Anthony's preaching! The experience most definitely got people's attention.

And his devotion to the Blessed Mother? Incredible! An article from EWTN.com shows that his love of the Virgin Mary started early:

> From the outset his life was markedly Marian, being born in Lisbon on the feast of the Assumption, August 15th, 1195 A. D., and baptized in the

Church of St. Mary in Lisbon. At the age of 15 he completed his studies at the Cathedral School of St. Mary. Appropriately his earthly life, ever pure and humble, was brought to a close in a similar Marian tone, for when death drew nigh he longed to be taken to the St. Mary, Mother of God Friary in Padua. After receiving Extreme Unction he intoned his favorite hymn, "O gloriosa Domina … " (O glorious Lady). He lived and died with the Virgin Mary on his lips and in his heart.

Keep this in mind as you remember that Saint Anthony is not just your go-to when you can't find your car keys, but also when you want to deepen your relationship with the Mother of God! And here's a prayer to Mary, composed by Saint Anthony that you should take a photo of and share on social media right now, because it's absolutely beautiful:

Mary, Our Queen
(a Marian prayer of Saint Anthony)

Mary, our Queen, Holy Mother of God, we beg you to hear our prayer. Make our hearts overflow with divine grace and resplendent with heavenly wisdom. Render them strong with your might and rich in virtue. Pour down upon us the gift of mercy so that we may obtain the pardon of our sins. Help us to live in such a way as to merit the glory and bliss of heaven. May this be granted us by your Son Jesus who has exalted you above the angels, has crowned you as Queen, and has seated you with him forever on his refulgent throne.
Amen.

Alphonsus Liguori

There is no possible way to overstate the incredible impact of Saint Alphonsus Liguori on the Church and the world. He lived from 1696 to 1787 and was an Italian Catholic bishop, in addition to being a writer, composer, musician, artist, poet, lawyer, philosopher, theologian, and founder of the Redemptorists.

Snap It! Have you completed the Total Consecration to Jesus Through Mary and do you wear the little chain around your wrist? Snap a photo of it and post it on Instagram!

It is clear that he loved the Blessed Virgin Mary, as he took the religious name Maria, but his love didn't stop there. Alphonsus preached Mary from the pulpit, and his Mariology was a profound challenge to the rationalism of the time that tried to downplay her importance.

The Glories of Mary, the book for which Saint Alphonsus is probably best-known, was written as a defense against the Jansenists, who criticized Marian devotion at the time. He opens the book with a deep explanation of the Hail Holy Queen prayer, continues with a rich description of the various Marian feast days, touches on Mary's sorrows and what he calls her "prolonged martyrdom," and closes with a discussion on Mary's ten principle virtues and particular prayers and devotions to help develop a relationship with her.

I guess he inspired my idea for this book without me even realizing it! Here's a prayer to Mary from this saint that you can snap a photo of and post with a filter to get everyone in on the action:

A Petition to Mary
(by Saint Alphonsus Liguori)
Most holy Virgin Immaculate, my Mother
Mary, to thee who art the Mother of my Lord,

the queen of the universe, the advocate, the hope, the refuge of sinners, I who am the most miserable of all sinners, have recourse this day. I venerate thee, great queen, and I thank thee for the many graces thou has bestowed upon me even unto this day; in particular for having delivered me from the hell which I have so often deserved by my sins. I love thee, most dear Lady; and for the love I bear thee, I promise to serve thee willingly forever and to do what I can to make thee loved by others also. I place in thee all my hopes for salvation; accept me as thy servant and shelter me under thy mantle, thou who art the Mother of mercy. And since thou art so powerful with God, deliver me from all temptations, or at least obtain for me the strength to overcome them until death. From thee I implore a true love for Jesus Christ. Through thee I hope to die a holy death. My dear Mother, by the love thou bearest to Almighty God, I pray thee to assist me always, but most of all at the last moment of my life. Forsake me not then, until thou shalt see me safe in heaven, there to bless thee and sing of thy mercies through all eternity. Such is my hope. Amen.

Thérèse of Lisieux

Speaking of people's favorite saints, the Little Flower definitely deserves a spot on our list of holy heroes who are best suited to walk with you in your growing devotion to Mary. Saint Thérèse only lived from 1873 to 1897, but her impact on the spirituality of Catholics in our day is absolutely incredible. Saint Thérèse

promoted her "Little Way," a spirituality focused on doing little
things with great love, all offered up to Christ.

While she only lived for twenty-four years, her autobiography, *The Story of a Soul*, changed the lives of countless Catholics,
and led to her being canonized just twenty-eight years after her
death. She was eventually declared a Doctor of the Church for her
profound understanding of putting our faith into practice.

After she became a Carmelite, Thérèse painted a picture of
a lily, meant to symbolize her soul, and above it painted a star
with the letter M for Mary, showering down rays into the open
petals of herself. She often called Mary her "heavenly gardener"
and showed her love of Mary in her autobiography. She recounts
that, before she began to write, "I knelt down before the statue of
the Blessed Virgin, which had given to my family so many proofs
of her maternal protection, and I begged her to guide my hand
and not allow me to write a single line that might displease her."

Devotion to Mary started early for Thérèse, as her family en-
sured that Mary had a place in the home. Thérèse's father, Saint
Louis Martin, prominently displayed a statue of the Immaculate
Conception, and it was the focus of the family's prayer life. Mary
was always seen as the family's queen, and so it should be with all
of our families if we want to count saints among our children like
Saints Louis and Zelie (Thérèse's mother) are able to do! Share
this prayer of the Little Flower by posting it for all to see, and if
you get a knock at the door within seconds of hitting "share," I'll
bet it's a bouquet of roses.

Marian Prayer of Saint Thérèse of Lisieux
Virgin full of grace,
I know that at Nazareth you lived modestly,
without requesting anything more.
Neither ecstasies, nor miracles,
nor other extra ordinary deeds

enhanced your life,
O Queen of the elect.
The number of the lowly,
"the little ones,"
is very great on earth.
They can raise their eyes to you without any
  fear.
You are the incomparable Mother
who walks with them along the common way
to guide them to heaven.
Beloved Mother,
in this harsh exile,
I want to live always with you
and follow you every day.
I am enraptured by the contemplation of you
and I discover the depths of the love of your
  heart.
All my fears vanish under your motherly gaze,
which teaches me to weep and to rejoice!
Amen.

Maximilian Kolbe

We talked about Saint Maximilian Kolbe and his devotion to Mary in chapter 6.

Here I just want to point out that, similar to Saint Louis de Montfort, Saint Maximilian Kolbe also gave us a path for consecrating ourselves to Jesus through Mary. His three-part consecration has helped many souls down through the years and solidifies him as one of the greatest Marian saints in our Church's long history.

The Immaculata Prayer of Saint Maximilian Kolbe

O Immaculata, Queen of Heaven and earth, refuge of sinners and our most loving Mother, God has willed to entrust the entire order of mercy to you. I, (name), a repentant sinner, cast myself at your feet, humbly imploring you to take me with all that I am and have, wholly to yourself as your possession and property. Please make of me, of all my powers of soul and body, of my whole life, death and eternity, whatever most pleases you.

Search This! Think you have a messy desk? Search for a picture of the desk of Saint Maximilian Kolbe and you'll instantly feel better! You'll also notice his statue of Mary. It's a meme-worthy photo. Just think about that!

If it pleases you, use all that I am and have without reserve, wholly to accomplish what was said of you: "She will crush your head," and "You alone have destroyed all heresies in the whole world." Let me be a fit instrument in your immaculate and merciful hands for introducing and increasing your glory to the maximum in all the many strayed and indifferent souls, and thus help extend as far as possible the blessed kingdom of the most Sacred Heart of Jesus. For wherever you enter you obtain the grace of conversion and growth in holiness, since it is through your hands that all graces come to us from the most Sacred Heart of Jesus.

V. Allow me to praise you, O Sacred Virgin.
R. Give me strength against your enemies.
Amen.

John Paul II

Saint John Paul II was the pope for the first twenty-three years of my life, so you can understand why I find him to be one of the most influential saints in recent history. When it comes to Marian devotion, few come close to his love of the Blessed Virgin. Born in 1920 in Poland, Karol Jozef Wojtyla was to become one of the most influential leaders of the twentieth century. His influence helped bring many home to the Catholic Church, impacted world governments, and brought the peace and love of Christ to the world in a way that hadn't been accomplished by any pope before him.

In 1987, he released the encyclical *Redemptoris Mater*, subtitled "On the Blessed Virgin Mary in the life of the Pilgrim Church." The document covers such topics as Mary's role in salvation history, the role of Mary as the Mother of God, and the role of Mary as mediatrix. It has references to Saint Louis de Montfort and provides a lot of beautiful food for thought about just how awesome the Blessed Virgin Mary is for our Church and each one of us personally.

At a general audience on November 15, 1995, JPII shared just how important Marian devotion is for the faithful: "It can be clearly seen ... how the Marian dimension pervades the Church's whole life. The proclamation of the Word, the liturgy, the various charitable and cultural expressions find in Mary an occasion for enrichment and renewal." He lived his life and his pontificate with that focus in mind, and just a few years later we have the opportunity to follow his lead and grow closer to her and her Son in a similar manner.

To You, O Mary
(written by Saint John Paul II)

O Mother of men and peoples, you know all their sufferings and their hopes, you feel in a motherly way all the struggles between good and evil, between the light and the darkness which shakes the world. Accept our cry addressed in the Holy Spirit directly to your heart and embrace with the love of the Mother and the Handmaid of the Lord the peoples who await this embrace the most, and likewise the peoples whose consecration you too are particularly awaiting. Take under your motherly protection the whole human family which we can consecrate to you, O mother, with affectionate rapture. May the time of peace and freedom, the time of truth, justice and hope, approach for everyone.

O you, who are the first handmaid of the unity of the Body of Christ, help us, help all the faithful, who feel so painfully the drama of divisions of Christianity to seek with constancy the way to the perfect unity of the Body of Christ by means of unconditional faithfulness to the Spirit of Truth and Love, which was given to them by your Son at the cost of the cross and death.

O you, who are so deeply and maternally bound to the Church, preceding the whole People of God along the ways of faith, hope and charity, embrace all men who are on the way, pilgrims through temporal life towards eternal destinies, with that love which the divine

Redeemer himself, your Son, poured into your heart from the cross. Be the Mother of all our earthly lives, even when they become tortuous, in order that we may all find ourselves, in the end, in that large community which your Son called the fold, offering his life for it as the Good Shepherd.

O you, who were with the Church at the beginning of her mission, intercede for her in order that going all over the world she may continually teach all the nations and proclaim the Gospel to every creature.

O you, who have known in the fullest way the power of the Holy Spirit, when it was granted to you to conceive in your virginal womb and to give birth to the Eternal Word, obtain for the Church that she may continue to give new birth through water and the Holy Spirit to the sons and daughters of the whole human family, without any distinction of language, race, or culture, giving them in this way the "power to become the children of God." [Jn. 1:12].

O you, who have always wished to serve! You who serve as Mother the whole family of the children of God, obtain for the Church that enriched by the Holy Spirit with the fullness of hierarchical and charismatic gifts, she may continue with constancy towards the future along the way of that renewal which comes from what the Holy Spirit says and which found expression in the teaching of Vatican II, assuming in this work of renewal everything that is true and good, without letting herself be deceived either in one direction or in the other, but discerning assiduously among the signs of the times what is useful for the coming of the Kingdom of God.

O you, who — through the mystery of your particular holiness, free of all stain from the moment of your conception, feel in a particularly deep way that "the whole creation has been groaning in travail" [Rom. 8:22], while, "subjected to futility," "it hopes that it will be set free from its bondage to decay" [Rom. 8:20–21], you contribute unceasingly to the "revealing of the sons of God," for whom "the creation awaits with eager longing" [Rom. 8:19], to enter the freedom of their joy [cf. Rom. 8:21].

O Mother of Jesus, now glorified in heaven in body and in soul, as the image and beginning of the Church, which is to have its fulfillment in the future age, here on earth, until the day of the Lord comes [cf. 2 Pt. 3:10], do not cease to shine before the pilgrim people of God as a sign of sure hope and consolation (cf. *Lumen Gentium*, 68).

O you, who more than any other human being have been consecrated to the Holy Spirit, help your Son's Church to persevere in the same consecration.

Holy Spirit of God, You who is worshipped and glorified with the Father and Son! Accept these words of humble consecration addressed to You in the heart of Mary of Nazareth, Your bride and mother of the Redeemer, whom the

Church too calls her Mother, because right
from the Upper Room at Pentecost she has
learned from Her, her own motherly vocation!
Accept these words of the pilgrim Church,
uttered amid toils and joys, fears and hopes.
Amen.

Find Your Own Squad

It would be an understatement to say that this chapter merely
scratches the surface of saints who loved the Blessed Virgin Mary
and had a strong devotion to her. If you feel particularly called to
one of the aforementioned saints, take some time to delve deeper
into their lives, their spiritual practices, and grow alongside them
in your own devotion to Mary. If you don't, look into other saints
who had a devotion to Mary that may better speak to you. The
point is to find your own path, your own journey that takes you
closer to her, and to find companions to walk alongside you who
have provided an example that resonates with you and your particular devotional life.

Search for saints you're interested in on your social media
app of choice and scroll through the posts about the saints, the
icons of them, the prayers they composed, and share your journey
with everyone as you delve deeper.

The squad is there, and they're waiting for you.

11

Pin-worthy Prayers

A collection of Marian devotions and prayers
to take you from level 1 to level ∞

L et's pray!
    If there's one thing I hope this book accomplishes, it's leading people to a deeper relationship with the Blessed Virgin Mary through prayer. With that in mind, I wanted to ensure that the final chapter of this book focused on precisely that: Marian prayers. Obviously, I want you to feel like you can pick up this book over and over again to reread it to your heart's content, but in particular, I want to leave you with a specific chapter you can flip to in a time of need and find solace by quickly being able to locate prayers that lead you into the peaceful embrace of the Mother of God.

    And so, without further ado, here is the compendium of Marian prayers that have impacted my life in powerful ways. I hope they bring you the same peace, the same hope, the same joy, and the same love that they bring me.

Ave Maria

Hail Mary,
full of grace,
the Lord is with thee.
Blessed art thou among women,
and blessed is the fruit
of thy womb, Jesus.
Holy Mary,
Mother of God,
pray for us sinners now,
and at the hour of our death.
Amen.

Memorare

Remember, O most gracious Virgin Mary, that never was it known that anyone who fled to thy protection, implored thy help, or sought thine intercession was left unaided.

Inspired by this confidence, I fly unto thee, O Virgin of virgins, my mother; to thee do I come, before thee I stand, sinful and sorrowful. O Mother of the Word Incarnate, despise not my petitions, but in thy mercy hear and answer me.

Amen.

Magnificat

My soul proclaims the greatness of the Lord,
my spirit rejoices in God my Savior
for he has looked with favor on his lowly servant.
From this day all generations will call me blessed:
the Almighty has done great things for me,
and holy is his Name.

He has mercy on those who fear him
in every generation.

He has shown the strength of his arm,
he has scattered the proud in their conceit.

He has cast down the mighty from their thrones,
and has lifted up the lowly.
He has filled the hungry with good things,
and the rich he has sent away empty.

He has come to the help of his servant Israel
for he remembered his promise of mercy,
the promise he made to our fathers,
to Abraham and his children forever.

Salve Regina

Hail, holy Queen, Mother of Mercy, our life, our sweetness and our hope. To thee do we cry, poor banished children of Eve. To thee do we send up our sighs, mourning and weeping in this valley of tears. Turn, then, most gracious advocate, thine eyes of mercy toward us, and after this, our exile, show unto us the blessed fruit of thy womb, Jesus. O clement, O loving, O sweet Virgin Mary.

V. Pray for us, O holy Mother of God.
R. That we may be made worthy of the promises of Christ.
Amen.

Litany of Loreto

V. Lord, have mercy.
R. Christ, have mercy.

V. Lord, have mercy. Christ, hear us.
R. Christ, graciously hear us.

God the Father of heaven, have mercy on us.

God the Son, Redeemer of the world, have mercy on us.
God the Holy Spirit, have mercy on us.
Holy Trinity, one God, have mercy on us.

Holy Mary, pray for us.
Holy Mother of God, pray for us.
Holy Virgin of Virgins, [etc.]

Mother of Christ,
Mother of divine grace,
Mother most pure,
Mother most chaste,
Mother inviolate,
Mother undefiled,
Mother most amiable,
Mother most admirable,
Mother of good Counsel,
Mother of our Creator,
Mother of our Savior,

Virgin most prudent,
Virgin most venerable,
Virgin most renowned,
Virgin most powerful,
Virgin most merciful,
Virgin most faithful,

Mirror of justice,
Seat of wisdom,
Cause of our joy,
Spiritual vessel,
Vessel of honor,
Singular vessel of devotion,

Mystical rose,
Tower of David,
Tower of ivory,
House of gold,
Ark of the covenant,
Gate of heaven,
Morning star,
Health of the sick,
Refuge of sinners,
Comforter of the afflicted,
Help of Christians,

Queen of Angels,
Queen of Patriarchs,
Queen of Prophets,
Queen of Apostles,
Queen of Martyrs,
Queen of Confessors,
Queen of Virgins,
Queen of all Saints,
Queen conceived without original sin,
Queen assumed into heaven,
Queen of the most holy Rosary,
Queen of families,
Queen of peace,

V. Lamb of God, Who takest away the sins of the world,
R. Spare us, O Lord.
V. Lamb of God, Who takest away the sins of the world,
R. Graciously hear us, O Lord.
V. Lamb of God, Who takest away the sins of the world,
Have mercy on us.
V. Pray for us, O holy Mother of God.

R. That we may be made worthy of the promises of Christ.

Let us pray. Grant, we beseech Thee, O Lord God, that we thy servants may enjoy perpetual health of mind and body, and by the glorious intercession of blessed Mary, ever Virgin, may we be freed from present sorrow, and rejoice in eternal happiness. Through Christ our Lord.

R. Amen.

Angelus

The Angel of the Lord declared unto Mary:
And she conceived of the Holy Spirit.

Hail Mary, full of grace, the Lord is with thee; blessed art thou among women and blessed is the fruit of thy womb, Jesus. Holy Mary, Mother of God, pray for us sinners, now and at the hour of our death. Amen.

Behold the handmaid of the Lord:
Be it done unto me according to Thy word.
Hail Mary …

And the Word was made flesh: [genuflect]
And dwelt among us.
Hail Mary …

Pray for us, O Holy Mother of God, that we may be made worthy of the promises of Christ.

Let us pray:
Pour forth, we beseech Thee, O Lord, Thy grace into our hearts; that we, to whom the incarnation of Christ, Thy Son, was made

known by the message of an angel, may by His passion and cross be brought to the glory of His resurrection, through the same Christ Our Lord. Amen.

The Seven Sorrows Devotion
1. The prophecy of Simeon (Lk 2:34-35)
2. The flight into Egypt (Mt 2:13-14)
3. The loss of the child Jesus in the Temple (Lk 2:43-45)
4. The meeting of Jesus and Mary on the Way of the Cross (Lk 23:27)
5. The crucifixion (Jn 19:25-27)
6. The taking down of Jesus from the Cross (Mk 15:43-46)
7. The burial of Jesus (Mt 27:57-60; Jn 19:40-42)

This devotion can be prayed as a Rosary, saying one Our Father and seven Hail Mary's for each of the seven sorrows. Or it can be prayed more simply, praying one Hail Mary and meditating on the Scripture verse for each sorrow.

Stabat Mater Dolorosa
At the Cross her station keeping
Stood the mournful Mother weeping,
Close to Jesus to the last.

Through her Heart, His sorrow sharing,
All His bitter anguish bearing,
Lo! the piercing sword had passed.

O how sad and sore distressed
Was that Mother, highly blessed,
Of the Sole-Begotten One.

Mournful, with Heart's prostration,

Mother meek, the bitter Passion
Saw She of Her glorious Son.

Who on Christ's dear Mother gazing,
In Her trouble so amazing,
Born of woman, would not weep?

Who on Christ's dear Mother thinking,
Such a cup of sorrow drinking,
Would not share Her sorrow deep?

For His people's sins rejected,
Saw Her Jesus unprotected.
Saw with thorns, with scourges rent.

Saw Her Son from judgement taken,
Her Beloved in death forsaken,
Till His Spirit forth He sent.

Fount of love and holy sorrow,
Mother, may my spirit borrow
Somewhat of your woe profound.

Unto Christ with pure emotion,
Raise my contrite heart's devotion,
To read love in every wound.

Those Five Wounds on Jesus smitten,
Mother! in my heart be written,
Deep as in your own they be.

You, your Savior's Cross did bear,
You, your Son's rebuke did share.

Let me share them both with Thee.

In the Passion of my Maker,
Be my sinful soul partaker,
Weep 'til death and weep with you.

Mine with you be that sad station,
There to watch the great salvation,
Wrought upon the atoning Tree.

Virgin, you of virgins fairest,
May the bitter woe Thou bearest
Make on me impression deep.

Thus Christ's dying may I carry,
With Him in His Passion tarry,
And His Wounds in memory keep.

May His Wound both wound and heal me,
He enkindle, cleanse, strengthen me,
By His Cross my hope and stay.

May He, when the mountains quiver,
From that flame which burns forever,
Shield me on the Judgement Day.

Jesus, may Your Cross defend me,
And Your Mother's prayer befriend me;
Let me die in Your embrace.

When to dust my dust returns,
Grant a soul, that to You yearns,
In Your paradise a place. Amen.

Act of Consecration

O Eternal and Incarnate Wisdom! O sweetest and most adorable Jesus! True God and True Man, only Son of the Eternal Father, and of Mary ever Virgin! I adore Thee profoundly in the bosom and glory of Thy Father during eternity; and I adore Thee also in the virginal bosom of Mary, Thy most worthy Mother, in the time of Thine Incarnation.

I give Thee thanks, that Thou hast annihilated Thyself taking the form of a slave, in order to rescue me from the cruel slavery of the devil. I praise and glorify Thee, that Thou hast been pleased to submit Thyself to Mary, Thy holy Mother, in all things, in order to make me Thy faithful slave through her. But alas! Ungrateful and faithless as I have been, I have not kept the promises which I made so solemnly to Thee in my baptism; I have not fulfilled my obligations; I do not deserve to be called Thy child nor yet Thy slave; and as there is nothing in me which does not merit Thine anger and Thy repulse, I dare no more come by myself before Thy Most Holy and August Majesty. It is on this account that I have recourse to the Intercession of Thy most holy Mother, whom Thou hast given me for a Mediatrix with Thee. It is by her means that I hope to obtain of Thee contrition, and the pardon of my sins, the acquisition and the preservation of wisdom. I salute Thee, then, O Immaculate Mary living tabernacle of the Divinity, where the Eternal Wisdom willed to be hidden and to be adored by Angels and by men. I hail thee, O Queen of heaven and earth to whose empire everything is subject which is under God.

I salute Thee, O sure refuge of sinners, whose mercy fails no one. Hear the desires which I have of the Divine Wisdom; and for that end receive the vows and offerings which my lowness presents to thee.

I, N. [Name], a faithless sinner — I renew and ratify today in thy hands the vows of my baptism; I renounce for ever Satan, his pomps and works; and I give myself entirely to Jesus Christ, the

Incarnate Wisdom, to carry my cross after Him all the days of my life, and to be more faithful to Him than I have ever been before.

In the presence of all the heavenly court I choose thee this day for my Mother and Mistress. I deliver and consecrate to thee as Thy slave, my body and soul, my goods, both interior and exterior, and even the value of all my good actions, past present and future; leaving to you the entire and full right of disposing of me, and of all that belongs to me, without exception, according to Thy good pleasure to the greatest glory of God, in time and in eternity.

Receive O gracious Virgin, this little offering of my slavery, in honor of, and in union with, that subjection which the Eternal Wisdom deigned to have thy Maternity, in homage to the power which both of you have over this little worm and miserable sinner, and in thanksgiving for the privileges with which the Holy Trinity hath favored thee. I protest, that I wish, henceforth, as thy true slave, to seek thy honour, and to obey thee in all things.

O admirable Mother, present me to thy Dear Son, as His eternal slave, so that as He hath redeemed me by thee, by thee He may receive me.

O Mother of mercy, get me the grace to obtain the true Wisdom of God, and for that end place me in the number of those whom thou lovest, whom thou teachest, whom thou leadest, and whom thou nourishest and protectest, as thy children and thy slaves. O Faithful Virgin, make me in all things so perfect a disciple, imitator and slave of the Incarnate Wisdom, Jesus Christ thy Son, that I may attain, by thy intercession and by thy example, to the fullness of His age on earth, and of His glory in heaven. Amen.

Regina Coeli

Queen of Heaven, rejoice, alleluia.
For He whom you did merit to bear, alleluia.
    Has risen, as he said, alleluia.

Pray for us to God, alleluia.

Rejoice and be glad, O Virgin Mary, alleluia.

For the Lord has truly risen, alleluia.

Let us pray:

O God, who gave joy to the world through the resurrection of Thy Son, our Lord Jesus Christ, grant we beseech Thee, that through the intercession of the Virgin Mary, His Mother, we may obtain the joys of everlasting life. Through the same Christ our Lord. Amen.

Prayer to Our Lady of Guadalupe

Our Lady of Guadalupe,

Mystical Rose,

make intercession for holy Church,

protect the sovereign Pontiff,

help all those who invoke you in their necessities,

and since you are the ever Virgin Mary

and Mother of the true God,

obtain for us from your most holy Son

the grace of keeping our faith,

of sweet hope in the midst of the bitterness of life

of burning charity, and the precious gift

of final perseverance. Amen.

Saint John Paul II's Prayer to Our Lady of Lourdes

Hail Mary, poor and humble Woman, Blessed by the Most High! Virgin of hope, dawn of a new era, we join in your song of praise, to celebrate the Lord's mercy, to proclaim the coming of the Kingdom and the full liberation of humanity.

Hail Mary, lowly handmaid of the Lord, Glorious Mother of Christ! Faithful Virgin, holy dwelling-place of the Word, teach us to persevere in listening to the Word, and to be docile to the voice of the Spirit, attentive to his promptings in the depths of our conscience and to his manifestations in the events of history.

Hail Mary, Woman of sorrows, Mother of the living! Virgin spouse beneath the Cross, the new Eve, be our guide along the paths of the world. Teach us to experience and to spread the love of Christ, to stand with you before the innumerable crosses on which your Son is still crucified.

Hail Mary, woman of faith, First of the disciples! Virgin Mother of the Church, help us always to account for the hope that is in us, with trust in human goodness and the Father's love. Teach us to build up the world beginning from within: in the depths of silence and prayer, in the joy of fraternal love, in the unique fruitfulness of the Cross.

Holy Mary, Mother of believers, Our Lady of Lourdes, pray for us. Amen.

Prayer to Our Lady of Perpetual Help

O Mother of Perpetual Help, grant that I may ever invoke thy most powerful name, which is the safeguard of the living and the salvation of the dying. O Purest Mary, O Sweetest Mary, let thy name henceforth be ever on my lips. Delay not, O Blessed Lady, to help me whenever I call on thee, for, in all my needs, in all my temptations I shall never cease to call on thee, ever repeating thy sacred name, Mary, Mary. Amen.

Children's Prayer to Mary

Dear Mother of Jesus,
look down upon me
As I say my prayers slowly
at my mother's knee.
I love thee, O Lady
and please willest thou bring
All little children
To Jesus our King. Amen.

Conclusion

"Ah, would that I could proclaim throughout the whole world the mercy that You have shown to me! Would that everyone might know I should be already damned, were it not for Mary! Would that I might offer worthy thanksgiving for so great a blessing! Mary is in me. Oh, what a treasure! Oh, what a consolation! And shall I not be entirely hers? Oh, what ingratitude! My dear Savior, send me death rather than such a calamity, for I would rather die than live without belonging entirely to Mary."

I have said these words every year since my very first walk through Saint Louis de Montfort's Total Consecration to Jesus Through Mary back in 2012, and the powerful nature of the prayer has never been lost on me.

From all eternity, it was the plan of the one true God that a humble girl from Nazareth would play a role infinitely more important than any creature before or any creature that will come after. Her yes — her "let it be done to me according to your word" — set in motion the offer of salvation for all mankind. For it was through her that God chose to bring His only begotten Son into the world. It was through her that God wanted to pour all of His grace and mercy into our lives. It was through her that God delivered the most important gift in all of human history.

And even better, Mary is not simply a person who lived two thousand years ago. God did not intend for Mary to be nothing more than a minor character in a dusty old story from a period of history we can hardly feel connected to anymore. Instead, she is a person we can have a relationship with right now. God intended for Mary to be your mother and mine, to walk with us on our faith journey as we try to grow ever closer to His Son and hers.

This is where social media comes in. We have an opportunity unlike any other in history, an opportunity to bring Christ to a world that so badly needs Him through a means that reaches people around the world instantly. We can share Christ and the Gospel with people online and potentially reignite the desire of people we will never meet in real life to live for Christ. And Mary wants to be a part of that journey.

We are meant to return to Jesus through the same means that God brought Jesus into the world: through Mary.

My relationship with Mary has been growing ever since I was a child, ever since my mother instilled a deep love of the Rosary in my heart, and quite frankly ever since I can remember. But the relationship hasn't stopped growing all these years later. Seemingly every day, I gain a new insight into the Blessed Virgin and her role in my life, the life of the Church, and the world as a whole.

My hope is that this book has planted even the tiniest of seed in your heart, a seed that will hopefully grow into a more incredible devotion to the Blessed Virgin Mary than you ever could have imagined. And I hope that you will take that growth and share it on social media, to inspire the world to turn toward Mary, trusting that she'll do the heavy lifting of inspiring the world to turn toward Him. If reading this book has encouraged you to say just one more Hail Mary, then I am happy. As the late Bishop Emeritus of Brooklyn Thomas Vose Daily once said, "The Power of One Hail Mary can change the world." Now imagine the power of asking everyone who follows you on social media to join together in that Hail Mary! So, you know, put down the book and pray one right now!

Acknowledgments

This book literally would not exist if not for the wonderful Sarah Reinhard, who reached out to me and asked if I had any interest in writing a book for the incredible team at Our Sunday Visitor. The idea certainly morphed over time, but ending up with a book all about Our Lady seems like a mighty fine way for things to have gone down.

I have to give a shout-out to my wonderful wife, Karen. Her support, guidance, and willingness to straight up tell me to delete things that didn't make any sense is the main reason why anything I write is any good at all. Her love, support, and partnership pull me along to heaven, no matter how resistant I may seem at times.

I don't think I would have nearly the imagination needed to write a book if not for my children: James, Paul, Andy, Luke, and Charlie! You five have changed my life in ways I never could have imagined before, and I have grown so much because of your love and example. You all keep me going, bring me joy, and challenge me to be better every single day. And it's just so much fun being your dad!

The team at Our Sunday Visitor deserve pretty much all the praise for this book! Mary Beth Baker is first and foremost among the team in terms of guiding me in the right direction and helping me every step of the way. Few know that book manuscripts pretty much make zero sense until the editor gets their hands on things, and this experience was no different! Thanks, Mary Beth!!

And lastly, I have to send every bit of hyperdulia I can muster to the Blessed Virgin Mary, the Mother of God, my mother, your mother, and the absolute crown of creation. The Queen of Heaven and Earth has carried me to her Son, kept her mantle wrapped tight around me, and walked with me through every joy and sorrow I have experienced. As Saint Louis de Montfort said, "Would that I could proclaim throughout the whole world the mercy that You have shown to me! Would that everyone might know I should be already damned, were it not for Mary!"

I can repeat those words of his without any hesitation.

"Mary is in me. Oh, what a treasure! Oh, what a consolation!"

About the Author

TOMMY TIGHE is the cohost of *Repent and Submit* on CatholicTV, the author of *The Catholic Hipster Handbook, Catholic Hipster: The Next Level,* and the coauthor of *How To: Catholic Family* and the *Catholic Funny Fill-ins* word game series with his wife Karen. He also hosts *Saint Dymphna's Playbook,* a weekly podcast on the intersection of mental health and Catholicism, for Grexly, a division of CatholicTV. He lives with his wife, Karen, and their family in the San Francisco Bay Area.